Lives and Legacies

Biographies in Western Civilization

Volume One

Jonathan S. Perry

University of South Florida

Upper Saddle River, New Jersey 07458

© 2009 by PEARSON EDUCATION, INC.
Upper Saddle River, New Jersey 07458

10 9 8 7 6 5 4 3 2 1

ISBN 10:   0-205-64915-7
ISBN 13: 978-0-205-64915-0

Table of Contents

Lives and Legacies

Biographies in Western Civilization

Volume One

Introduction

The Athenian Thucydides, one of the creators of the discipline called 'history' in the 5th century BCE, is said to have observed, 'History is philosophy taught by examples.' It was a vigorous debate in the Greco-Roman world whether 'biographical' writing could be compared to historical writing. The most famous ancient biographer, Plutarch (c. 46-120 CE), introduced his *Parallel Lives* of Alexander the Great and Julius Caesar with the warning that he was doing biography and not history. Therefore, he would write about the personal details that illuminate these important characters, and not give detailed descriptions of all of their battles. Nevertheless, Plutarch deliberately paired his 'Lives', one from the Greek world and one from the Roman, in order to draw a philosophical point: certain quirks of character can be found in various people, and those quirks can have similar consequences.

It may not seem obvious at first glance, but this book is also driven by a 'philosophy' of sorts. This is, to put it bluntly, the belief that the lives and experiences of individual persons 'matter', or should matter, to historians. By studying—or even better, as in Plutarch's own approach, by comparing—individual biographies, we believe we can come closer to understanding the historical epoch in which these individuals were born, conquered, loved, thought, created, murdered, and/or died.

Each of the biographies in this book is introduced with a series of questions designed to target your reading, and each concludes with suggestions for further research. As you read, consider especially the sources of evidence upon which these narratives have been built. Here's a disturbing thought along these lines: Would anyone really have been taking notes on someone in his/her early life, knowing that s/he *would be* famous, due to some twist of fate many decades down the road? Is it fair of us, therefore, to expect any account of the childhood years of our subjects to be completely reliable? This may become a particularly challenging point, when we attempt to determine the formative influences that 'made him what he was' or to make some other sententious declaration. Do human beings really work that way? Aren't we all, even today, a jumble of complexities and inconsistencies?

These very brief biographies, generally under 1000 words each (which, by the way, has been an enormous challenge to the authors, given how many more details could yet be added) are meant to be chewed slowly and savored. We hope you will find the subjects compelling enough to warrant further investigation, especially in the supplemental readings that have been assigned in your course. You should also pay close attention to the comparisons that have been made in each chapter. Why might a historian have chosen these two individuals to illustrate a common theme? What do these individuals, when taken together, reveal about the period in which they lived?

One final question to ponder: If a historian from the year 2750 visited us, asking which two individuals best illustrated our own time, whom would you suggest as the most appropriate? Given the 6.5 billion or so choices that will be available to this historian, it would certainly be a difficult decision.

Jonathan S. Perry

1
Chapter

Ancient Kingdoms:
Law and Religion

Hammurabi

The most famous of the Amorite kings of Babylon, Hammurabi is renowned primarily for his code of laws, though he also contributed to the rising influence and power of the kingdom of Babylon. What does the "Code of Hammurabi" tell us about Babylonian society?

* * *

One of the enduring controversies about Hammurabi, who was born in a village near the city of Babylon, has been the dates of his reign. In the course of the previous century, historians have placed him in several eras between the twenty-fourth century BCE and the nineteenth century BCE. Currently most scholars appear to have settled on the date noted above. Some sources place his birth around 1810 BCE, suggesting that he was young but mature when he succeeded as king in 1792 BCE. Babylon was at that time one of two Mesopotamian kingdoms, together with Assyria, that had emerged in the second millennium BCE to supplant the collapsed Akkadian Empire. Hammurabi was the sixth king of the first Babylonian dynasty, succeeding his father, King Sin-muballit.

Upon his accession, Hammurabi confronted considerable regional instability. Two other Amorite kingdoms, Eshnunna and Larsa, struggled with Babylon for dominance in the area. Perpetually shifting alliances between the three kingdoms and the uncertain loyalties of the smaller states made for a volatile political and diplomatic situation. Accordingly, Hammurabi's initial fame stemmed from his military successes. For nearly four decades, Babylon was engaged in intermittent warfare against neighboring powers, often against states that were previously allies.

3

Consequently, official histories depict Hammurabi as a great warrior, "the destroyer of his foes, the hurricane of battle." Ultimately he gained Babylon's independence and conquered territories sufficient to bring together a significant empire in northern Mesopotamia.

Hammurabi's achievements extended beyond military victory and conquest, however. When not engaged in war, Hammurabi dedicated resources toward significant construction projects. Canals, so vital to the distribution of water, were dug. Temples were constructed or restored, as were cities. Recognizing the importance of agriculture, Hammurabi took care to encourage and support it. His reign was also accompanied by significant literary and cultural activity. He did nothing, however, to alter the basic character of government. The prevailing conception of kingship held that the king personally oversaw virtually every aspect of government administration. The collection of revenue, the regulation and distribution of food, public works and every other conceivable duty of government were overseen by the king.

The accomplishment that stands above all these is, however, Hammurabi's codification of law, the earliest legal code known in its entirety. A French expedition discovered the stele containing the "Code of Hammurabi" at Susa (then in Persia) in December 1901. The stele is an obelisk-shaped block of black diorite slightly over seven feet in height and nearly seven feet in circumference at the base. The upper tip holds a large relief carving representing the king receiving the law from the sun god Shamash, affirming the divine origin of the written law and the quality of justice, which Shamash represents. The stele is covered with forty-four horizontal columns of cuneiform text, some 3800 lines. An inscription indicates that the stele was intended for the temple of Shamash at Sippar and that another copy stood in the temple of Marduk in Babylon. The existence of additional fragments suggests that there were likely similar steles in other cities. The existent stele was taken from Sippar in 1120 BCE, claimed as war booty by the Elamite King Shutruk Nahhunte. Though this stele, which now resides in the Louvre in Paris, was found in three pieces, it was restored to its original form.

The text of the inscription on the stele is divided into three parts. The first is an introduction, in which Hammurabi both proclaims the authority for and objectives of his rule. Describing Babylon as "an everlasting kingdom whose foundations were firm as heaven and earth," the text declares that the gods "called me, Hammurabi, the exalted prince, the worshiper of the gods, to cause justice to prevail in the land, to destroy the wicked and the evil, to prevent the strong from oppressing the weak...to enlighten the land and further the welfare of the people." The text continues to proclaim Hammurabi as "the governor...who brought about plenty and abundance; who made everything for Nippu and Durilu complete; who gave life to the city of Uruk; who supplied water in abundance to its inhabitants;" who made the city of Borshippa beautiful...who stored up grain for the might Urash." Ultimately, the introduction establishes Hammurabi as "the governor of the people, the servant, whose deeds are pleasing to Anunit." As immodest as the multitude of claims may seem, they provide a relatively accurate account of Hammurabi's domestic accomplishments and reflect an astute understanding of the chief political realities faced by any ruler – accomplishments mean little unless one receives adequate credit for them.

The main body of the code, comprising twenty-eight paragraphs, includes 285 laws. They begin with directions for legal procedures and a statement of penalties for unjust accusations, false testimony and injustice carried out by judges. Next follow laws arranged logically in categories of personal property, real estate, trades and business, the family, injuries and labor. Many reflect startling modern legal concepts, such as those that imposed penalties for injuries caused by unsuccessful medical procedures and for damages resulting from neglect in the trades. Fees for trade and commercial services are set in the code. The code also deals very specifically with such personal areas as marriage, adultery, divorce and women's property. Those portions of the code dealing with criminal law proscribe punishment on the basis of "equal retaliation," which in some cases necessarily meant severe penalties. A surgeon who ineptly blinded his patient, thus preventing him from any future gainful employment, might, for example, suffer the loss of his fingers, thus depriving him of his livelihood. While containing no laws relating to religion, the Code of Hammurabi is an extraordinarily comprehensive body of law meant to incorporate "the principles of truth and equity" and ensure protection of the weak from the strong.

The greatest number of laws, however, concerned property rights, especially those relating to rented lands, trade and commerce. The code imposed severe penalties for crimes against property, such as theft, fraudulent sales or negligent construction. Private commerce and property ownership were increasingly commonplace in Mesopotamian civilization in this era. It may well be that the Code of Hammurabi was as much in response to the need for uniform and equitable contract and business law as it was to any demand for general social justice. Though the code was far more humane than the laws of most societies at this point, its humanitarian qualities were inconsistent, and it preserved the class and gender inequities of the age. Free men who killed commoners were only fined, whereas commoners were executed; women could divorce their husbands only for cruelty, whereas men could gain a divorce for any reason.

The Code of Hammurabi, it appears, was probably at most a general guideline for legal affairs in Babylon. Records suggest that penalties meted out often were less severe than the code stipulated; judgments were often rendered by the people themselves, who gathered in courts to hear cases and make their own determinations. The key to the purpose of the code may be found in the text's conclusion, in which Hammurabi's greatness as a ruler is asserted in a succession of declamatory sentences hailing "the righteous laws" of the "wise king" who brought "pure government." "I am the guardian governor," the text proclaims, "in my bosom I carried the people of the land of Sumer and Akkad....in my wisdom I restrained them, that the strong might not oppress the weak, and that they should give justice to the orphan and the widow." The concluding text suggests that Hammurabi's Code was to a large extent the realization of the king's effort to demonstrate to the sun god that he has properly fulfilled the responsibilities of a divinely appointed monarch. Having provided for his people, Hammurabi could rest assured that he had performed his duties as expected. He died in 1750 BCE and was succeeded by his son Sumsuiluna.

Suggested Readings

Oates, Joan. *Babylon.* (1986).
Roux, Georges. *Ancient Iraq.* (1992).

Akhenaten (Amenhotep IV)

*Akhenaten, also known as Amenhotep IV, revolutionized Egyptian religious prac-
tice by elevating the cult of Aten above the numerous other Egyptian gods, thereby establishing, some historians argue, the first monotheistic religion. He introduced other
reforms during his reign, but Egyptians returned to their traditional religious beliefs
following his death. He is considered by some to be the last important ruler of the eigh-
teenth dynasty. Why was Akhenaten unsuccessful in permanently establishing the new
cult of Aten?*

* * *

Amenhotep IV, later Akhenaten, was the youngest son of Amenhotep III, a
pharaoh who brought Egypt to new heights of cultural and architectural achievement during a reign of forty years. There is some evidence that Akhenaten may have
reigned as co-regent during the latter years of his father's rule. Initially, Akenaten's
reign appeared to maintain continuity with the past. He was crowned at Karnak in
the temple of the god Amun and took as his throne name Nefer-kheperu-re ("Beautiful are the manifestations of Ra"). He chose a non-royal wife, Nefertiti, the daughter of a vizier, destined to become one of the most famous Egyptian queens.

Akhenaten is best known for his religious reforms, most notably his establishment of the cult of Aten, the sun god or solar disk. His motivations in doing so were
at least partly political; his father had grown increasingly concerned about the
power of the priesthood of Amun and had attempted to curb it. By introducing a
new monotheistic cult of sun worship, Akhenaten considerably reduced the authority of the potentially troublesome priests. There is some indication that Akhenaten
may also have been offended by the impieties of the priests, who were known to
maintain harems for their private amusements at the temples. The first major step
towards creating the new cult occurred in the second year of Akhenaten's reign, with
new constructions dedicated to Aten at Karnak. Akhenaten moved rapidly to re-
place the cult of Amun with that of Aten, a god accessible only to Akhenaten himself. This removed the need for any intermediaries such as priests. The cult of Amun
was soon proscribed, its temples closed and revenues confiscated.

A second crucial step in establishing the new cult of Aten was the founding of
a new capital. In the fourth year of his reign, Akhenaten announced the site of the
new sacred city, ostensibly "revealed by Aten himself," and the following year the
court moved there from Thebes. Designated as Akhenaten, or "Horizon of the Sun
Disc," the new city (now el-Amarna) was situated in a natural amphitheater created

by cliffs along the banks of the Nile River. The city was delineated by a series of 15 stele carved in rock around the perimeter. The steles depict Akhenaten, together with his wives and daughters, worshipping the sun god. The city was designed around a broad thoroughfare known as the "King's Road," which connected the two ends of the site; various official buildings, ceremonial constructions and living quarters lined the road. The centrality of the Pharaoh and his god Aten was to be reflected in both the architecture and life of the new city; everything that lived and prospered did so because of the pharaoh's patronage and Aten's benevolence.

Established in his new city, Akhenaten went about defining the nature of the new cult, which some commentators have described as the earliest monotheistic religion. Akhenaten altered all of his official names to reflect the new primacy of Aten. He also emphasized the worship of the visible aspect of the sun, the disc, the rays of which could be seen as a tangible manifestation of the creator. This made Aten more comprehensible to the common man, who could now see a physical manifestation of the divine. This was in considerable contrast to the cult of Amun, which could only offer a "hidden" god. To further enhance the power of his kingship and the cult, Akhenaten strove to establish a personal connection with Aten that would endow the pharaoh with the aspects of the creator, transforming the Sun-disc itself into a heavenly pharaoh by writing its name in a cartouche akin to his own. The pharaoh, accordingly, was the earthly representative of the creator, the "beautiful child of the Aten."

Akhenaten's religious reforms evidently had little impact on the Egyptian population. This was in part because the royal court had removed to Akhenaten and did not generally venture beyond the city's confines. Only the new temple at Karnak offered the public any conception as to the nature of the new royal cult. Also, the new cult reflected nothing of the traditional structure of the Egyptian society. Most were content to continue traditional religious beliefs and practices. Only among the upper classes was there much enthusiasm for the new cult and what existed may well have been superficial.

Akhenaten's reforms had much greater impact on politics, economics and art. The closure of proscribed temples, the confiscation of priestly wealth and the subsequent restriction of the role of the priesthood was attended by centralization of administrative and military authority. Local government was marginalized, with the result that problems went unmet while corruption and arbitrary actions increased. The construction of the new capital and the new temples was expensive, and the removal of the court from Thebes led to economic decline in that city.

Amidst these dislocations, art in all its forms nonetheless flourished. The new cult of Aten opened a path to greater freedom of expression in literary works, such as poetry. Egyptian sculpture from this era reflects a move away from the formality of earlier periods, as both a new realism and a willingness to experiment with exaggeration became evident. Perhaps the most famous example is the painted limestone bust of Nefertiti (now in a Berlin museum), depicting an elegant woman with an elongated neck and narrow skull. Some of the statuary of Akhenaten represents the king with exaggerated or even distorted features, leading to speculation about his androgynous appearance. While some experts suggest that it is simply an extreme example of artistic license, others theorize that Akhenaten's unusual physiognomy (long, narrow skull, large head on a long neck, fat accumulation in areas more typical of women than men) may have been the result of a medical condition, perhaps a tumor of the pituitary gland.

During the first decade of Akhenaten's reign, the young king succeeded in maintaining at least the appearance of success. He was evidently happy with his wife, who bore him six daughters, but no son. In the twelfth year of his reign, however, Nefertiti evidently fell out of favor, for reasons that remain unclear. Her place in official functions was taken by one of her daughters, though she apparently remained in the city until her death two years later. By the latter years of his reign, Akhenaten faced growing problems. The economic dislocations caused by the removal from Thebes generated some discontent. Additionally, the public in general had never embraced the new cult of Aten, and there were many who were offended by Akhenaten's efforts to physically erase reminders of Egypt's tradition polytheistic religion from public monuments. External pressures compounded matters as Hittites and other tribes threatened Egyptian dependencies in the Near East. When Egyptian-appointed governors requested troop reinforcements, Akhenaten hesitated. Though he was firm in his conviction that those areas should remain Egyptian, he was reluctant to commit his forces to such distant fields. Deprived of any substantial support from Egypt, governors could not enforce tributary payments and were soon deposed as subject peoples asserted their independence. Even as the Egyptian empire shrank, revenue collections in Egypt fell off drastically, due in part to increasingly incompetent administration.

There is some evidence that in the last two years of his reign, Akhenaten ruled jointly with Smenkhkare, probably his younger brother. When Akhenaten died in 1334 BCE, he was broadly unpopular and his successor did not long outlive him. Akhenaten's son-in-law, Tutankhamun, succeeded to the throne in 1334 BCE. Within two years, he began the process of dismantling the cult of Aten and restoring the old religion. The capital was returned to Thebes and the brief experiment in monotheism was soon forgotten.

Suggested Readings

Grimal, Nicholas. *A History of Ancient Egypt* (1992).
Johnson, Paul. *The Civilization of Ancient Egypt* (1978).

Chapter 2

Poets in Early Greece: 'Homer' and Sappho

'Homer'

While it is unclear whether he existed at all, or was only one person, 'Homer' exerted a profound influence on Greek, and then on Western, civilization. What does his work reveal about the way memory is distorted over time, to conform to new realities? Is written transmission of culture necessarily preferable to a story that is spoken or sung aloud?

* * *

The first line of the *Odyssey* reads, 'Sing to me, Muse, of the *polytropos* man.' Homer, and perhaps the Muse who inspired him, thus described Odysseus, the subject of his tale, as being 'of many twists and turns', 'of many wiles', 'changeable', 'devious', 'sneaky', or some other set of meanings, but the Greek word '*polytropos*' could also be applied to Homer himself. The biographical details related to the author of the epic poems *Iliad* and *Odyssey* have been subjected to many centuries of speculation, but the essential points are still in doubt.

At least seven different islands and cities were identified as his homeland, but most are roughly situated on the western coast of today's Turkey, in a region known to the Greeks as 'Ionia'. The poems are written in a dialect of Greek that was spoken in this region, by those Greeks who had sailed there from mainland Greece and the islands of the Aegean Sea. A historian of the 5th century BCE claimed that Homer had not lived more than four centuries before him, and historians today typically accept that 'Homer'—if he was, indeed, one individual—lived at some point in the 9th century BCE. The tradition of his having been blind is also highly debatable, the main evidence being another poem, later attributed to Homer but probably not his creation, entitled *Hymn to the Delphic Apollo*. The author of this work mentions that he is 'a blind man' who dwells on 'rugged Chios', an island off the shore of Asia Minor. Thus, in ancient times, 'Homer' was generally thought to have been a blind singer of songs who lived on the Ionian coast at a very early point in Greek history.

Today, by contrast, it is more common to see 'Homer' as the culmination of a series of poets who sang songs of heroic individuals in the past, generally accompanied by a stringed instrument called a lyre. According to this reconstruction, poems would have been sung, memorized, and subtly transformed by bards who did not write them down. In the 10th, 9th, and early 8th centuries BCE, Greece was experiencing a 'Dark Age', in which literacy—which had only been available to elite scribes assigned to the palace complexes of the Minoan and Mycenaean civilizations of the 2nd millennium BCE—had utterly disappeared. Because this poetry was transformed by 'word of mouth', it was known as 'epic' poetry, based on the Greek word 'epos' (originally 'wepos', until the 'w' sound dropped out of the language.)

Thus, we should read the epic poems as survivals dating to multiple periods of time. While they claim to chronicle events related to the Trojan War (of about 1200 BCE), it is more likely that they reflect the lived realities of the Dark Age, many centuries later. They are the logical products of a diminished, constricted, and meager time—we should envision Homer's original audience sitting around a campfire, with the region's lord living in a glorified hut and not in a grand palace, surrounded by animals and not by Trojan warriors, and on the verge of starvation, rather than dining on sumptuous banquets set before a distinguished guest. In these circumstances, it should be no surprise that the stories became richer, more sophisticated, and more detailed over time. Then, at some point, probably after 750 BCE, the epics began to take the form in which they are familiar to us. Through contact with the Phoenicians, another Mediterranean people that was expanding into the wider world at the same time, the Greeks adopted and adapted an 'alphabet'. The epic poems, which had previously been transmitted orally, were now set down in writing, and became fixed and frozen in that form.

Historians currently believe that each of the two man survivals of this tradition, the *Iliad*, of more than 16,000 verses, and the *Odyssey*, of about 12,000, was the work of a single individual, but it is not clear whether the same person composed both pieces. This is due, in part, to the essential differences in theme and approach between the two poems. The *Iliad* develops its theme of the 'wrath' of Achilles, in the final year of the 10-year-long Trojan War. While it chronicles various duels and glories in the details of stomach-churning gore and eyeballs exploding upon being speared, its most moving sections suggest the human cost of war, and the suffering of Greece's enemies is given as much attention as that of the Greeks. The *Odyssey* continues the story of the War, following one of the Greeks in his 10-year journey back to his home, his son, and the wife whom he had left behind two decades earlier. Here, the poet addresses the theme of hospitality. In short, it is good manners to treat a guest with dignity, provide a meal and entertainment, and exchange gifts. It is bad manners to show up in someone's house uninvited, camp out there for many years, and harass his wife—and probably worse to *eat* a guest who has mistakenly wandered into one's cave.

With his stirring narratives, rich psychological insight, and sense of wonder at deeds done by gods and men in a glorious past, Homer became one of the cornerstones of Greek identity and culture. He is sometimes mistakenly called the 'Bible' of the Greeks, but it is more appropriate to call him their 'Shakespeare', fusing Greek-speakers who lived in many different places and had a multitude of different political allegiances into a shared cultural unit. And he can still command big box office returns—if in barely recognizable form—after nearly 3000 years.

Suggested Readings:

The Iliad, translated by Robert Fagles, introduction and notes by Bernard Knox, New York: Viking, 1990.
The Odyssey, translated by Robert Fagles, introduction and notes by Bernard Knox, New York: Viking, 1996.

Sappho

Sappho occupies a unique place in Western Civilization. Her poetry contributed to the development of Greek culture in the 'Archaic' Age, and her life illuminates the potential of at least some Greek women to break out of the conventional restrictions of a deeply misogynistic culture. What subjects might have seemed more appropriate to lyric than to epic poetry? Does Sappho's poetry subvert or undermine 'Homeric values'?

* * *

Homer began both of his epics by appealing to a Muse for assistance, and the Greeks generally acknowledged nine of these goddesses in their myths. However, the philosopher Plato said there should be a tenth, a human and actual woman who lived on the island of Lesbos between the late seventh and early sixth centuries BCE. Sappho is important for many reasons, and not only for the beauty and profound impact of her poetic work—she is one of the very few women whose distinct voices survive, even in this fragmentary form, from ancient times, and thus she begins, in very small measure, to counteract the gender imbalance that is obvious in most of Western history. Because her name has, though indirectly, been applied to expressions of erotic passion between women, a study of her life and experiences also casts light on the variety of sexual relationships and attachments that existed in previous eras.

Despite her significance, in both artistic and personal terms, the details of Sappho's life are, like those of Homer's, shrouded in mystery. Most of what we know about her can be gleaned from her poetry itself. She seems to have spent most of her life in the city of Mytilene, on the island of Lesbos in the northern Aegean Sea. Ancient writers suggested an array of possible birthdates for her, but most of these place her birth between 650 and 600 BCE. There are a number of fanciful stories concerning her death, at least one of which was designed to suggest that her principal erotic attachments were to men.

While this seems not to have been the case, judging from the passionate terms in which she addresses other females in her poetry, Sappho was probably married to a man, and presumably one of her own elevated class background. While a husband is not mentioned, Sappho was especially proud of her daughter, named Cleis ('Brilliant'), who is celebrated in one of the surviving poems. She also mentions a brother, and, because she was literate and of some political importance in the community, she must have been a member of an upper-class family. Prominence came at a price, though: at least once, and perhaps a second time, she was exiled from Mytilene due to her family's political connections.

Very little of Sappho's total poetic output has survived, but nearly 200 fragments (some very tiny) have been identified, collected, and translated from the original Greek. She seems to have been highly regarded in antiquity, but her poetry suffered a fate similar to that of many other poets, male and female, in the Middle Ages. In periods of general chaos and dislocation, the entire literary production of many authors was deliberately destroyed, accidentally lost in fires or other disasters, or else simply not preserved in enough copies to survive to the present day. Luckily, Sappho's work was transferred to many papyrus copies in Egypt, and new fragments of her poetry periodically appear. (The two most recent were made available in 2001 and 2005.)

The surviving work exemplifies a new sort of poetry called 'lyric', as opposed to the 'epic' tradition represented by Homer. Probably also accompanied by the lyre, lyric poetry tends to shy away from grand battles and the schemes and squabbles of the gods, focusing instead on small human interactions, celebrating the thoughts, experiences, and loves of us mere mortals. For example, Sappho, in her most famous poem, describes her pounding heart, humming ears, and sweaty hands when she hears the voice of a woman she loves, and she declares, in another piece, that the most beautiful thing in the world is not a corps of cavalry, a line of soldiers, or a flotilla of ships, but instead the person one loves. In this poem, as well, she expresses her sympathy for Helen, who inadvertently began the Trojan War by following her heart to Troy. (Men had typically castigated Helen's weakness and unfaithfulness to her husband, by contrast.)

Her frank depiction of homoerotic passion led later generations to label this sort of passion 'sapphic' or 'lesbian', in honor of Sappho and her home island. We cannot now determine how common this sort of expression was in Lesbos, or in other Greek cities, at this time, but it is clear that Sappho felt no need to hide her feelings, and no religiously-inspired shame in naming her attractions. In a series of poems, she celebrated the weddings of the young women to whom she had addressed other pieces. At the very least, her work illustrates that erotic passion can come in many forms, and that love can inspire beautiful work, in any time period.

Suggested Readings:

Anne Carson, *If Not, Winter: Fragments of Sappho*, New York: Knopf, 2002.
Margaret Williamson, *Sappho's Immortal Daughters*, Cambridge: Harvard University Press, 1995.

3

Chapter

Greek Historians

Herodotus

Called "the Father of History" by Cicero, Herodotus became the first chronicler to gather his documents systematically, seek to ascertain their veracity, and offer a thoughtful and lively narrative. It was Herodotus who employed the word "historie," which had stood for research, to explain how he was providing a record of human development. Herodotus became most noted for the nine volumes he produced on the emergence of the Persian Empire, the Persian assault into Greece, and the subsequent Greek triumph. What kind of achievement did Herodotus attain? How authentic were his tales?

* * *

The historian Herodotus was born in the first or second decade of the fifth century BCE at Halicarnassus in the southwestern sector of Asia Minor, then part of the Persian empire. Queen Artemisia ruled Halicarnassus, later leaving her throne to her son Pisindelis, who in turn was succeeded by Lygda as Herodotus reached manhood. Herodotus's family, including his father Lyxes, who was probably from Caria, and his mother, whose name was either Rhaeo or Dryo, was stationed in the upper social strata. He had one brother, Theodore, and another relative, Panyasis, who was an uncle or a cousin, and an esteemed poet.

Herodotus undoubtedly received the liberal education that comfortable Greek citizens did: grammar, gymnastics, and music. When he turned eighteen, he took his place among Halicarnassus's *ephebi* or *eirenes*, the young men who were undergoing military training. However, he possibly felt stifled, due to the tyrannical rule that his home city endured. Thus, he may have opted to follow the lead of Panyasis in becoming a writer. Clearly, he undertook an extensive reading program poring over the works of Homer, Hesiod, Ovid, Lysistratus, Sappho, Solon, Aesop, Aeschylus, and Pindar, among others. He particularly referred to Hecateus, up to that point considered the finest Greek prose writer.

Fearing that Panyasis was engaged in treasonous activities, the despot Lygdamis had him sentenced to death around 457 BCE. Herodotus, who apparently shared the political perspectives of Panyagis and appeared to be involved in the attempt to oust the ruling dyasty, was either compelled to depart from Halicarnassus or left of his own accord as the execution was taking place. Herodotus sailed for the Ionian island of Samos, which was a key component of the Athenian confederacy. His family's comfortable economic status, perhaps coupled with the felt need to distance himself from Halicarnassus, led to extensive travels, both in Greece and in other lands. Most of those travels were apparently conducted between 464 and 447 BCE, although some date them later. Herodotus went through much of Asia Minor and European Greece, visiting islands of the Archipelago-Rhodes, Cyprus, Crete, Italy, Sicily, Sparta, and Athens, among other spots. He traveled from Sardis to Susa, the Persian capital, went to Babylon, and spent considerable time in Egypt, which was at the time largely influenced by Athens.

Following the ouster of Lygdamis, which Herodotus may have participated in, Halicarnassus became a willing participant in the Athenian confederacy. Herodotus evidently returned to his native city, where his history was beginning to receive an initial, unfavorable response. That probably convinced him to leave Halicarnassus once again and to seek refuge in Athens—the center of intellectual life in Greece—around 447 BCE. There, Herodotus was treated with great favor, even being awarded the generous sum of ten talents, thanks to a decree by the citizens of that city-state. Herodotus was seen in the company of his friend Sophocles, when he was in Athens. Among the other noteworthy intellectual figures to be found in that Greek city-state were Pericles, Thucydides, Protagoras, Zeno, Olorus, Antiphon, Euripides, and Sophocles. Herodotus was certainly close to Sophocles, Thucydides, and Olorus, among others.

But Herodotus chose not to remain in Athens, where an elevated status was hardly afforded writers, unless they performed other tasks as well. Socrates, for example, was an infantryman; Sophocles commanded naval fleets; and Thucydides served as a general in the Greek army. In addition, Herodotus must have been aware that the franchise, so valued by free Greeks, was not easily attained. Thus, it is hardly surprising that he chose to sail with a group of colonists who, in 444 or 443 BCE, established the colony of Thurii, which Pericles championed. He later referred to himself as Herodotus of Thurii, which included as one of its colonists, the great philosopher, Pythagoras.

It was possibly the outbreak of the Peloponnesian War between Athens and Sparta in 431 BCE that induced Herodotus to construct his story of battles, historical developments, and travels as a full narrative. Herodotus's own fame results from his nine volume *Histories*, which displayed a bounty of information about fifth century BCE Persia and Greece. At the outset, Herodotus explained that he wrote these books to preserve "from decay the remembrance of what men have done" and to keep "the great and wonderful actions of the Greeks and the Barbarians from losing their due of glory." The *Histories* related the emergence of the Persian Empire, but also provided accounts of Lydia, Media, Assyria, Babylon, Egypt, Scythia, and Thrace. Included were descriptions of landscapes and the people who inhabited them, as well as climatic factors. In addition, Herodotus discussed the history of the people of Greece, examining their colonies, political machinations, wars, religion, and more.

This collection provided, in effect, the initial history produced by the Western world. As the historian Margaret L. King notes, Herodotus, who died in approximately 425 BCE, differentiated the West from the East. He considered the Persian Wars of the early fifth century BCE the defining moment of his age, when Greek city-states repulsed twin invasions from massive armies.

Shortly after the publication of Herodotus's *Histories*, his work was considered path-breaking. Writers had previously produced chronicles and epic tales, in their efforts to record the past. However, Herodotus was the first to examine the past in philosophical fashion and to conduct research to track human behavior. The *Histories* proved highly controversial throughout the ancient era, and its author was condemned for his purported biases and inaccuracies. However, in the past several decades, Herodotus has been lauded as a pioneer in history, ethnography, and anthropology. His lyrical style, acknowledged by contemporaries and later generations alike, continues to be appreciated. Cicero termed his prose "copious and polished," while Quintilian called it "sweet, pure and flowing."

Suggested Readings

Herodotus, *The Histories* (1999).
Lateiner, Donald. *The Historical Method of Herodotus*, 1992.
The Greek Historians: The Essence of Herodotus, Thucydides, Xenophon, Polybius, ed. Moses I.
Finley (1977).

Thucydides

Another great Greek historian, Thucydides is best known for his History of the Peloponnesian War, an epic battle waged between Athens and Sparta that occurred during the latter stages of the fifth century BCE. Thucydides took extraordinary care to verify the authenticity of the stories he relayed, turning to many key surviving participants on both sides. He also offered remarkable presentations of orations, such as one delivered by Pericles. How is Thucydides's work distinguished from that of Herodotus? What contributions did Thucydides offer the historical discipline?

* * *

Thucydides was born around 460 BCE into a prominent Athenian family, which owned gold mines at Scapte Hyde on the Thracian coast opposite Thasos. His father Olorus was related to the Thracian prince, whose daughter Hegesipyle was wedded to Miltiades, who helped to defeat Darius I at Marathon; Cimon was the son of Hegesipyle and Miltiades. Family wealth afforded Thucydides two dwelling places: one in Athens and the other in Thrace; moreover, the family gold mines undoubtedly led to Thucydides's frequent stays in Thrace, where he must have been involved with overseeing those invaluable resources. In addition, the connections his relatives possessed enabled him to meet powerful men who were shaping history in their own fashion. Undoubtedly, during his early schooling, Thucydides was educated by Sophists, who taught rhetoric, philosophy, and critical thinking.

Prior to the outbreak of the Peloponnesian War in 431 BCE, Thucydides evidently played no major role in Athenian political affairs. That conflict arose as the might of the Athenian Empire proved threatening to many other Greek states, including Sparta, which proved troubled by Athens's naval supremacy and its control of key ports along the Aegean Sea. As Thucydides indicated, "What made the war inevitable was the growth of Athenian power and the fear which this caused Sparta." Early during the war, the plague swept through Athens, afflicting Thucydides, along with many of his fellow citizens. Later, he indicated that "he had seen others suffer" and had apparently helped minister to his fellow citizens. In 424 BCE, he was named *strategos* or a general in the Athenian military. While commanding the area near Thrace, Thucydides arrived to ward off a Spartan attack by Brasidas on Eion, but proved unable to help save Amphipolis, which had stood as an Athenian stronghold in the northwest. As a consequence, he suffered condemnation, probably instigated by Cleon, and forced exile for a period of seven years.

For much of the remainder of the war, as he resided at his property in Thrace, Thucydides determined to write about it, believing that no other event in the recorded history of Greece, not even the Trojan War or the Persian Wars, could match its importance. Athens and Sparta were vitally important Greek city-states, with highly contrasting worldviews. The intellectual and artistic influence of Athens on other Greek cities was considerable, as was Sparta's martial emphasis. Moreover, non-Hellenic peoples in Thrace, Macedonia, Epirus, Sicily, and the Persian Empire were affected by political and cultural developments in Greece. Thucydides hoped to accurately track the Peloponnesian War itself, but also to provide lessons for future generations. A faithful history, he believed, would serve "those who desire an exact knowledge of the past as a key to the future, which in all probability will repeat or resemble the past. The work is meant to be a possession for ever, not the rhetorical triumph of an hour." To those ends, he painstakingly gathered evidence and interviewed participants. That required extensive travels, and he readily visited allies of the warring parties. The war itself, Thucydides reasoned, was a disastrous affair, resulting from "love of power operating through greed and through personal ambition."

Thucydides hoped to surpass the contributions of previous students of Greek history, including Homer and Herodotus. Epic poets like Homer had waxed eloquent about their subjects, but had deliberately melded together fable and fact. The Ioanian prose writers or chroniclers, seeking a popular audience, had uncritically sought to record tales of legend. Thucydides, for his part, refused to blame the gods or fate for historical events. In contrast to Herodotus, whom he apparently lumped with the Ionian chroniclers, Thucydides made every effort to ascertain the veracity of the materials he obtained. Thucydides indicated, "My account rests either on personal knowledge or on the closest possible scrutiny of each statement made by others. The process of research was laborious, because conflicting accounts were given by those who had witnessed the several events, a partiality swayed or memory served them." At the same time, he clearly drew his own interpretations about the origins of the conflict and how it unfolded, and was hardly remiss in expressing his viewpoint. In presenting his history, which largely excluded social, artistic, and literary occurrences, Thucydides nevertheless attempted to make it readable. He generally succeeded, as when he offered graphic descriptions of the plague's impact on Athens or his account of the fateful Sicilian campaign.

Among the most noteworthy aspects of Thucydides's *History of the Peloponnesian War* were his reconstructions of political addresses, some of which he heard during the first stages of the conflagration. He explained his approach in incorporating these orations: "As to the speeches made on the eve of the war, or in its course,

I have found it difficult to retain a memory of the precise words which I had heard spoken; and so it was with those who brought me reports. But I have made the persons say what it seemed to me most opportune for them to say in view of each situation; at the same time I have adhered as closely as possible to the general sense of what was actually said." The best known of these is the Funeral Oration delivered by Pericles in honor of those who had perished on the Athenian side. In eloquent fashion, Pericles discusses the greatness, freedom, and democracy of Athens.

> Our system of government does not copy the institutions of our neighbors. ... Our constitution is called a democracy because power is in the hands not of a minority but of the whole people. When it is question of settling private disputes, everyone is equal before the law; when it is a question of putting one person before another in positions of public responsibility, what counts is not membership of a particular class, but the actual ability which the man possesses. ... Then there is a great difference between us and our opponents, in our attitude toward military service. ... Our city is open to the world ... we rely, not on secret weapons, but on our own real courage and loyalty. ... Taking everything together then, I declare that our city is an education to Greece. ... This, then, is the kind of city for which these men, who could not bear the thought of losing her, nobly fought and nobly died. Its greatness derives from the freedom of its citizens.

Another remarkable aspect of the *History of the Peloponnesian War* involved Thucydides's discussion of the conquest of Melos. His "Melian dialogue" conveyed Thucydides's perception that "the strong do what they have the power to do and the weak accept what they have to accept." Demosthenes, the great orator, explained how a city-state could be governed by equitable laws and customs, unlike affairs between states, where the strong invariably dominated the weak.

At the conclusion of the Peloponnesian War, Thucydides returned to Athens for a brief period, before Lysander's takeover. He then retired to his estate in Thrace, remaining there until his death, continuing to work on his grand history of the war that had so crippled the great Greek city-states. He apparently died around 400 BCE, at which point his remains were sent to Athens and placed in the vault of Cimon's family. His sudden death explains why his history ends abruptly in 411 BCE, seven years before the war came to a close. The *History of the Peloponnesian War* was enthusiastically read by Demosthenes, while Cicero and Quintilian were reportedly influenced by it as well. Thucydides appeared to have recognized how important his contribution was, asserting that he was recording "the greatest movement yet known in history, not only of the Hellenes but of a large part of the barbarian world."

Suggested Readings

Thucydides. The Peloponnesian War. Terry Wick, ed. (1982).
The Greek Historians: The Essence of Herodotus, Thucydides, Xenophon, Polybius. Moses I. Finley, ed. (1977).

4

Chapter

Athens' Leaders at War:
Themistocles and Alcibiades

Themistocles

The ideal product of the new Athenian 'democracy', Themistocles led his city to victory against the Persian King when Greece was invaded in 480 BCE. However, he fell to the whims of the 'demos' ten years later, and died in what might seem an odd place. What does his life reveal about the strengths—and the weaknesses—of 'people power'?

* * *

Homer had celebrated Odysseus for being '*polytropos*', and the people of Athens would come to celebrate (and then turn on) two living examples of this quality in the 5th century BCE. The first was Themistocles, remarkable during his lifetime and for many centuries afterward for being '*sunetos*': clever, intelligent, and (a bit) devious. Athens' savior at Salamis—and in the preparation for the battle in the 480s—Themistocles was the subject of much writing in antiquity, including a biography by the 1st-century-CE Plutarch, and extensive coverage in the histories of Herodotus and Thucydides. It may be the case that his career could have been achieved nowhere except Athens, which, after 510, was experimenting with a new form of government based on and exercised by 'the people'.

Themistocles was, by common judgment, born into an obscure and unimportant Athenian family (and his mother was probably not Athenian.) He did not have the benefit of the standard, expensive aristocratic education, but he gained a reputation for being naturally clever and an extremely effective speaker. Luckily for Themistocles, the new democracy had opened up avenues for people like him—the best politicians in Athens were those who could persuade their fellow citizens in the *ekklesia*, or popular Assembly. Because Athens was a direct, and not a representative, democracy, the only thing required was to persuade a majority of the people to support a measure. The way was, accordingly, thrown open to those who could manipulate popular enthusiasm for unscrupulous, as well as for legitimate, purposes.

Managing to have himself elected *archon* in 493, Themistocles witnessed, and presumably participated in, the Battle of Marathon in 490, in which the Athenians fought off a Persian landing force in Attica, against all expectations. While others rejoiced in their miraculous victory over the mightiest empire in the world, Themistocles was clever enough to look ahead to the future. He reasoned that the Persians, the masters of many dozens of restive subject peoples in the Middle East, would not tolerate a humiliation like this without response. Thus, he began planning for the second round of war with Persia, which he believed would come at some point.

And then came a lucky strike—literally, as a rich vein of silver was found in Laurion in Attica in 483. As per the conventions of the democracy—and with the usually willing cooperation of self-interested politicians—everyone expected the proceeds from this mine to be divided among the Athenian citizenry. Themistocles, by contrast, whipped up patriotic enthusiasm against one of Athens' regional rivals, suggesting that it was in the state's best interest to invest this windfall in a fleet of warships. Amazingly, Themistocles managed to carry the day, and 'trireme' construction began—just in time, he reasoned, to provide a suitable force against Persia, the real enemy for which he was preparing.

An inscribed text found only in 1959 helps confirm the idea that Themistocles was also formulating another master stroke of strategy, i.e. the evacuation of Athens itself, should the Persians threaten the city, and placing the city's full confidence in its navy. When the Persians did launch their invasion in 480, under the leadership of King Xerxes I, Themistocles wisely yielded command of a united Greek force to the Spartans, and began making plans for the next stage of the war. When the Spartans went down in a heroic, but ultimately unsuccessful, stand at Thermopylae in northern Greece, Themistocles ordered a mass evacuation of the city, with women, children, and the elderly transplanted to a safe spot and every man of military age transplanted to the newly-constructed ships. The Athenians watched in horror as the Persians looted and burned their city, but then Themistocles made his most important contribution to the effort. Amassing Athens' ships in the very narrow straits of Salamis, Themistocles sent a messenger to Xerxes, insinuating that he was prepared to betray his fellow citizens, and that Xerxes should attack the Athenians with his big and bulky ships early the following morning.

Xerxes took the bait—presumably because he had heard that Themistocles was a wily and self-centered politician—and his ships went down to a humiliating defeat at Salamis on 29 September 480. Athens repelled the invaders, and all of the Greeks lauded Themistocles for his clever and innovative strategies against the enemy. However, immediately after this war had ended, the seeds for the next, the Peloponnesian War, were sown. The Spartans encouraged the Athenians not to rebuild their walls, but to rely, instead, on Spartan protection in the future. Themistocles understood the truth of this ruse, and delayed the Spartans with false promises. When the walls had been surreptitiously rebuilt, a newly fortified Athens was presented as a fait accompli—but at the expense of a brief moment of cooperation among the fiercely independent Greek city-states.

Subsequently, Themistocles fell victim to the mechanisms of democracy and his enemies—and, perhaps, to his own greed. In 470, he was accused before the citizens for taking bribes and lining his pockets with the contributions of Athens' new allies. Whether this was true or not, he was ostracized by his fellow citizens (and a number of 'ostraka', potsherds on which his name was scratched, have survived, either from this or some earlier ostracism.) After wandering around Greece for some years, Themistocles finally took refuge with—of all people—the King of Persia, either Xerxes himself or his son Artaxerxes I, who succeeded to the throne in 465. The night he received Themistocles under his protection, the Persian reportedly sacrificed to the gods, drank himself to sleep, and cried out three times during the night, 'I have Themistocles the Athenian!' Themistocles never returned to Athens. He died, with much respect and honor among his former enemies, at the age of 85.

Suggested Reading:

Barry S. Strauss, *The Battle of Salamis: The Naval Encounter that Saved Greece—and Western Civilization,* New York: Simon and Schuster, 2004.

Alcibiades

Alcibiades was also, in his own way, a logical product of Athenian democracy. Extremely handsome, rich, and reckless, he cut a unique path through Greek politics in the course of the Peloponnesian War. This war dominated the second half of the 5th century, as the Persian Wars had dominated the first. In what specific ways might the lives of Themistocles and Alcibiades be compared? What does Alcibiades' career suggest about the potential vulnerabilities of a democratic system?

* * *

Alcibiades was yet another in that long series of Greek heroes who lived by their wits, playing both ends against the middle, but then were forced to pay heavy price for so doing. He inspired the passions of some of the most prominent aristocrats, philosophers, and artists of his day, but he also knew how to stir up the love of the mass populace of Athens. He was the subject of a series of biographies and accounts, including a Life by Plutarch, extensive coverage in the histories of Thucydides and Xenophon, and several appearances in the dialogues of Plato. He was also the butt of jokes in the developing dramatic form of 'comedy', and his deeds inspired wonder in his fellow Athenians and those who followed them.

Alcibiades was born to a very distinguished family, on both his father's and mother's sides, and his mother's family included Cleisthenes, the founder of Athens' democracy. Unfortunately, his father died soon after his birth, and Alcibiades grew up in the home of Pericles, who served as the boy's guardian. He could hardly have found a more opportune location, learning from a political master how to take and hold power, and how to wield it effectively. While Alcibiades grew up, Pericles channeled his energies, and those of his people, into massive building projects, playwriting, sculpture—and an aggressive foreign policy that would eventually plunge Athens and her allies into war with Sparta and her allies, in 431 BCE.

As a young man, Alcibiades took part in the first phase of the Peloponnesian War, called the Archidamian (431-421). This war ended with the Peace of Nicias, a truce between the two warring powers that was supposed to last 50 years. (It ultimately lasted, with interruptions, about five.) In this period, the attractive and wild-living Alcibiades cut a prominent figure in what was still a small city. Alcibiades was ardently pursued by both men and women, inspiring passions but then, usually, spurning their advances. On one occasion, however, it seems that he went out of his way to seduce Socrates, who was famous for possessing a brilliant mind, but also for being old and ugly. Socrates had had a series of relationships with handsome young men, and Alcibiades was reportedly shocked and irritated that Socrates refused to yield to his advances.

However, Alcibiades was eventually married to Hipparete, who finally grew so tired of his dalliances with other partners that she rushed to the center of Athens, determined to secure a divorce. Plutarch claims that Alcibiades discovered her plans, followed her, picked her up, and carried her back to their house. Hipparete died (coincidentally?) shortly afterward. Another tale claims that, when he was accused in a law case by a political rival, Alcibiades strode into the sacred precincts where lawsuits were registered, licked his finger, and erased the indictment, which had been inscribed on a wax tablet.

Alcibiades' moment of fame came in 415, when the Athenians were debating sending aid to an ally in far-away Sicily. While cooler, older, and perhaps wiser heads advised against intervention, Alcibiades threw caution to the wind, insisting that this was an ideal opportunity for Athens to expand the war and conquer a new, and very rich, part of the world for its Empire. So effective was his speech (he made effective use of his own remarkable victories in the chariot race at the Olympics of 416) that, Thucydides notes, everyone was wild with enthusiasm for what was certain to be a short and profitable war. Those who disagreed, he adds ominously, kept their mouths shut, for fear of seeming 'unpatriotic'.

The Sicilian Expedition was launched, therefore, but it would end in catastrophic defeat within two years. Alcibiades, however, took another path, due to a series of incidents that immediately preceded the launch of the fleet to Sicily. The morning the ships were to leave, the city's 'herms', statues whose only features were a head and an erect phallus, had been 'mutilated' [the details are not difficult to imagine....] It is probably not surprising that, given his reputation for recklessness and impiety, Alcibiades and his friends were accused of this outrage—and further charges of his mimicking and ridiculing certain religious ceremonies were added to the mix. Facing conviction—he was eventually tried in absentia and his property confiscated by the government—Alcibiades jumped ship off the coast of Italy. He then surfaced in, of all places, Sparta, Athens' greatest enemy.

Feeling rejected by his city, Alcibiades aided the Spartans but eventually found it too risky to stay there: he had seduced and, perhaps, fathered the child of the Spartan Queen. He continued his traitorous tour of the region by dealing with the Persians, who hoped to exploit Greek divisions for their own purposes, and by also keeping in contact with former friends in Athens, who had their own grievances against the democracy.

Nevertheless, it was a renewed democracy (after the short-lived coup of a group of 'oligarchs' in 411) that called Alcibiades back to be its leader. Once again, Alcibiades demonstrated that he was an effective commander, if not an altogether trustworthy one, and Athens began to win again. But, given the fickle nature of the populace, Alcibiades fell out of favor yet again and went into exile in 406.

Athens ultimately lost the war to the Spartans in 404, and then Alcibiades was murdered, although the identity of his assassins is in doubt. Perhaps the lesson of his life is: Keep your options open, and don't burn bridges. You may need to walk across them again one day.

Suggested Readings:

Walter M. Ellis, *Alcibiades,* London: Routledge, 1989.
Donald Kagan, *The Peloponnesian War,* New York: Viking Penguin, 2003.

5

Chapter

The Roman Era:
War and Expansion

Scipio Africanus

One of the greatest Roman generals, Scipio Africanus defeated Hannibal in the Second Punic War. For nearly two decades, Hannibal had threatened key parts of the Roman Empire, including the capital city itself. Throughout much of that period, Scipio, fighting on two continents, battled against Hannibal's forces, eventually confronting the Carthaginian military genius himself in North Africa. How crucial was Scipio's triumph? What would a Carthaginian victory have prevented from taking place?

* * *

Publius Cornelius Scipio Africanus was born in either 236 or 235 BCE, the son of Publis Cornelius Scipio, a member of one of Rome's oldest and most respected patrician families. Livius indicates that Scipio, from his fourteenth birthday, never conducted any business without first stopping at the temple of Jupiter on the Capitol. Scipio's father, following family tradition, was a Roman consul who had been sent to head the Roman forces in Spain; Scipio accompanied his father on this venture. Having reached Massila, the elder Scipio discovered that Hannibal had reached the Rhone. Hannibal had opened the Second Punic War by attacking the Spanish city of Saguntum, a Roman ally situated south of the Ebro River. Along with 30,000 men, Hannibal crossed the Alps into Italy. Publis Cornelius Scipio sent his troops on to Spain but returned to Italy to head the Roman forces gathered in the Po Valley. Scipio again joined his father, as the Cathaginians and the badly outnumbered Romans met at the River Ticinus.

Through the battle of Ticinus, where his uncle Gnaeus Cornelius Scipio also fought, Scipio began to acquire his own reputation as a military mastermind. His father, who was seriously wounded, and a number of his soldiers confronted a large group of Cathaginian cavalrymen. Scipio implored another Roman contingent to rescue their encircled compatriots. When none agreed to do so, Scipio recklessly undertook the dangerous mission on his own. His embarrassed soldiers finally followed his lead, breaking the Carthaginian formation, thereby enabling the elder Publis Cornelius Scipio to be freed. His father ordered that Scipio be awarded the *corona civica*, the greatest military commendation that a Roman soldier could receive, but the young man refused, declaring, "The action was one that rewarded itself." He was soon elected a military tribune and became engaged to Aemilia, the daughter of Aemilius Paullus, another Roman general.

Scipio survived another fight with Hannibal that took place in Cannae, where thousands of soldiers fled in panic during the midst of a devastating defeat that saw 50,000 Romans perish. At the conclusion of the debacle, the remnants of the Roman forces selected Scipio and Appius Claudius as their commanders. They received word that a mutiny was being planned in Rome, talk of which led a number of young nobles to consider heading overseas. Scipio urged calm, declaring, "Courage and action, not deliberation, are necessary in such a calamity." Along with a few colleagues, Scipio helped to thwart the plot, exclaiming, "I swear that I will neither desert the cause of Rome, nor allow any other citizen of Rome to desert it." The terrified plotters gave up, taking an oath of allegiance instead.

In 214 BCE, Scipio, still only twenty-two years old, was named an *aedile*, as was his cousin Lucius Cornelius. Two years later, he suffered the loss of both Publis Cornelius Scipio and Gnaeus Cornelius Scipio, who died in battles in the Baetis Valley in Spain; they had gone there to reign in Iberian tribes that had backed the Carthaginian army and to tackle Hannibal's forces in Spain, who were stationed along the Spanish coast in New Carthage. Following their setback, less than 10,000 legionnaires controlled the Ebro line in the face of three of Hannibal's armies, numbering 45,000 soldiers.

No senior Roman general desired to avenge the killings of their peers or to punish Iberian tribes that had gone over to Hannibal's side; they considered the risks of failure and ensuing ignominy were too great. Still too junior an officer to be placed in command of an imperial station, Scipio, in an unprecedented move, sought support from the *populi* or Roman citizens. In 211 BCE, having been elected proconsular imperium of Spain, Scipio, leading an army of 10,000 infantrymen and 1000 cavalrymen, departed from Rome. He was ordered to prevent Carthaginian forces from gaining more ground in Spain and from sending reinforcements to assist Hannibal in Italy. Scipio, however, determined to follow his father's lead and push the Carthaginians out of Spain altogether. Drawing on his analysis of Hannibal's operations in Italy, Scipio turned to the cohort, a smaller group of infantrymen, which afforded improved maneuverability. He also placed Spanish swords, rather than the more unwieldy ones the Romans employed, in the hands of his soldiers. In 210 BCE, Scipio, now boasting 25,000 foot soldiers and 2500 men on horseback, traversed the Ebro. Marcus Silanus and 3500 men were left to control the river. Scipio further divided his army, sending contingents by sea to New Carthage and beginning a 325 mile march that took a full week to complete. The fighting proved fierce but was not prolonged before Scipio was able to take New Carthage, inducing the Carthaginians to retreat to Gades. In 209 BCE, Scipio went against the army headed by Hasdrubal Barca, Hannibal's brother, near Baecula. Again departing from conventional Roman military strategy, Scipio split up his own forces and used his lighter armed troops as a diversionary ploy to enable his main units to attack Hasdrubal Barca from the side. The badly defeated Hasdrubal Barca managed to escape but was killed by Roman troops at the Metaurus River. At the Battle of Ilipa in 206 BCE, Scipio pummeled the remaining Carthaginian forces, which were led by Hasdrubal, the son of Gisgo. Subsequently, the final Carthaginian stronghold at Gades was taken, completing the Roman conquest of Iberia, which would last for seven centuries.

Scipio, for his part, was now named a Roman consul. Not content with the successes he had experienced, Scipio sought permission from the Roman Senate to attack North Africa. Such an invasion, he presumed, would compel Hannibal to halt his sixteen-year-long assault against Italy, or, at a minimum, cut off any means of support for the Carthaginian general from his homeland. Many in the Senate proved reluctant to grant Scipio his request, allowing him to go only to Sicily but not providing any military forces. In Sicily, Scipio formed a volunteer army and continued to seek permission to strike at Carthage. That decision was reached in 204 BCE, and Scipio prepared to strike. He sent Gaius Laelius on an ambassadorial mission to Africa to carve out an alliance with Syphax and Masinissa, two Numidian chiefs who were chafing at Carthaginian control. Unconvinced, Masinissa attacked Laelius instead, compelling him to flee into the desert. Numidian cavalry forced Scipio to abandon his initial foray into north Africa, along the coast at Utica. Following the defeat of Syphax and his Cathaginian allies in a pair of battles, however, Masinissa decided to switch sides. Before Scipio departed from Sicily, he prayed to "ye god and ye goddesses, who inhabit the seas and the lands ... to grant us the power to take revenge upon our enemies and foes; and that you will grant to me and the

Roman people the power to enforce the Carthaginians what they have planned to do against our city, as an example of [divine] punishment."

In 203 BCE, Scipio's forces crushed a Carthaginian army near Utica, killing 40,000 and capturing 5000 others. With the assistance of Gaius Laelius and Masinissa, Syphar and the Numidians were defeated at the battle of Great Plains. Beseeched to return home, Hannibal soon met Scipio in a famous encounter that featured only two others—their interpreters--but then the two great generals confronted one another on the battlefield. At Zama in 202 BCE, Scipio, once more using unconventional tactics, routed Hannibal's army and returned in triumph to Rome, where he delivered over 120,000 pounds of silver to the Senate and was given the name *Africanus* because of his victory. In 199 BCE, he was elected a censor, which required him to supervise the census and to safeguard public morals. Five years later, he was chosen a consul for a second time, and then was selected as *princeps senatus* for a third occasion in 189 BCE, leading to his defeat of King Antiochus at Magnesia in 189 BCE.

Controversy, however, soon beset Scipio and his famous family. Enemies, including Cato the Elder, accused his brother Lucius and Scipio himself of taking bribes. In front of the tribunal, Scipio shredded documents attacking his brother. Then, Scipio confronted charges by Marcus Naevius that he had afforded King Antiochus easy terms because of a large bribery payment. When the Senate demanded that he appear before it to face corruption charges, Scipio refused to heed the summons. Instead, he retired to his country estate, located at Liternum. He came to the rescue of his old rival, Hannibal, when Romans sought to capture and enslave the great Carthaginian general. Ironically but perhaps fittingly enough, both Scipio and Hannibal died in 183 BCE: Hannibal by his own hand, and Scipio declaring that the ungrateful citizens of Rome were not entitled to bury him.

Suggested Readings

Hart, B. H. Liddell and Michael Grant. *Scipio Africanus: Greater Than Napoleon* (1994).
Livy. *Scipio Africanus: The Conqueror of Hannibal* (1987).

Cleopatra VII

Remembered perhaps most of all for her ill-fated love affairs with Julius Caesar and Marc Antony, Cleopatra VII served for over two decades as Queen of Egypt. Her reign, which ended in 30 BCE, brought to a close the Ptolemy dynasty established three centuries earlier. Following her suicide, Egypt became part of the Roman Empire. An important historical figure, Cleopatra passed into the realm of legend thanks to stories spun about her by Shakespeare, Dryden, and Shaw, among others. Why has Cleopatra caught the imagination of so many historians and artists alike? How important was her reign for Egypt?

* * *

Cleopatra VII was born in Alexandra, the capital of Egypt, in 69 BCE, the oldest child of King Ptolemy XI Auletes. Her mother was reputedly Cleopatra V Tryphaena, Auletes's sister, such bonding was a common practice for royal families in Egypt. The family was Macedonian, with its members descendants of Ptolemy I, who had served as a general under Alexander the Great. After Alexander's death in 323 BCE, Ptolemy became satrap of Egypt and later proclaimed himself king. Along with her siblings, Cleopatra became aware that Julius Caesar was battling their guardian, Pompey, in a civil war that wracked Rome. When her father died in 51 BCE, the seventeen year-old Cleopatra and her twelve year-old brother Ptolemy XIII jointly succeeded to the throne, provided that they married. She served as Queen Philopator and Pharaoh, ruling virtually alone for the first three years. However, in 48 BCE, Ptoltemy's advisers, including the eunuch Pothinus, were angered by Cleopatra's independence and seized the reins of government, forcing her into exile. Her sister Arsino joined her in Syria.

Residing there, Cleopatra collected an army but didn't act until Julius Caesar arrived in Alexandria. Having been defeated by Caesar at Pharsalus, Pompey had gone to the Egyptian capital, seeking support from Ptolemy. The king's advisers reasoned, however, that it would be more advisable to back Caesar and thus they had Pompey murdered. Caesar, to his dismay, was confronted with his former friend's head when he appeared. Consequently, his men took over the palace and ordered Ptolemy and Cleopatra to meet with Caesar. Fearing that she would be killed if discovered in Alexandria, Cleopatra was delivered to Caesar, wrapped up in an oriental rug. Caesar, who quickly became Cleopatra's lover, soon championed her cause. Although hardly beautiful in any classical sense, the politically deft Cleopatra was apparently both highly charismatic and seductive, boasting a lovely musical voice as well. She was quite intelligent, was mathematically-inclined, and possessed business acumen. Reputed to have spoken nine languages, Cleopatra was the first pharaoh in the Ptolemy line to speak Egyptian.

After Ptolemy was arrested, his army attacked the palace. Striving to appease the angry Egyptians, Caesar called for Ptolemy's release. Nevertheless, the Alexandrian War continued on for approximately six months, concluding with the death of both Pothinus and Ptolemy. After Alexandra surrendered, Caesar proclaimed Cleopatra queen of Egypt. Required to marry her eleven year-old brother Ptolemy XIV, Cleopatra parted with Caesar for an extended boat ride along the Nile. Following the cruise, Caesar departed for Rome but left three legions behind to protect his lover. Cleopatra's son and probably Caesar's, Caesarion ("little Caesar")—who became Ptolemy XV—had been born in Alexandria. In 46 BCE, mother, child, and Ptolemy XIV left for Rome to reside in a palace Caesar had constructed for them.

In Rome, Caesar was granted numerous honors and a dictatorship that was slated to last ten years. His open declaration that Caesarion was his son, coupled with his apparent determination to wed Cleopatra, although he was already married, enraged many Romans. So did his intention to declare himself king. Thus, on the Ides of March in 44 BCE, Caesar was assassinated by Senators, including his good friend Marcus Brutus. Fearing that her life was also in danger, Cleopatra returned to Egypt, where she had Ptolemy murdered, so that her son could rule alongside her. A triumvirate was established between Antony, Marcus Lepidus, and Gaius Octavius, Caesar's adopted son.

In 42 BCE, Antony invited Cleopatra, whose land was nearing economic collapse, to visit him in Tarsus. She went attired as Venus, the goddess of love, which clearly appealed to Antony, an unsophisticated man of lusty appetites. Plutarch, the great Greek writer, said of Cleopatra,

Plato admits four sorts of flattery, but she had a thousand. Were Antony serious or disposed to mirth, she had at any moment some new delight or charm to meet his wishes; at every turn she was upon him, and let him escape her neither by day nor by night. She played at dice with him, drank with him, hunted with him; and when he exercised in arms, she was there to see. At night she would go rambling with him to disturb and torment people at their doors and windows, dressed like a servant-woman, for Antony also went in servant's disguise... However, the Alexandrians in general liked it all well enough, and joined good-humouredly and kindly in his frolic and play.

Antony and Cleopatra spent that winter together in Alexandria. Cleopatra convinced him to assassinate her sister Arsinoe, who had turned against her. Six months following Antony's departure, Cleopatra had twins, Cleopatra Selene and Alexander Helios; four years would pass before Cleopatra saw Antony again. In the meantime, Antony married Octavia, the half-sister of Octavian.

In the midst of a campaign to subdue the Parthians, Antony sent for Cleopatra. When she arrived in Antioch, he officially recognized their twins and ceded her considerable territory, including Cyprus, Phoenicia, Judea, Arabia, and the Cilician coast. The latter land provided Egypt with the timber necessary to construct a large fleet. In the meantime, Antony suffered a military defeat in 36 BCE, which made Cleopatra—whom he had married and who had just had their third child, Ptolemy Philadelphus—more indispensable to him than ever. In 34 BCE, Antony conducted a far more successful campaign against Armenia.

Antony's relationship with Cleopatra enraged many of his countrymen, who were appalled that the couple referred to themselves as gods: the New Isis and the New Dionysus. Then, in 34 BCE, Antony named Alexander Helios, Cleopatra Selene, and Ptolemy Philadelphus, the rulers of Armenia, Cyrenaica and Cyrus, and Syria, respectively. Cleopatra was declared the "Queen of Kings," and Caesarion, the "King of Kings." Her favorite oath was "As surely as I shall yet dispense justice on the Roman Capital." In 32 BCE, after Octavian declared war against Cleopatra and Antony, the latter divorced his Roman wife. Cleopatra participated in the military campaign, but withdrew her fleet when she believed Antony's defeat was certain at Actium in 31 BCE. The two fled to Alexandria, where Antony, having heard that Cleopatra had killed herself, committed suicide. Worried that Octavian intended to transport her back to Rome in chains, Cleopatra then took her own life, perhaps with an asp.

Cleopatra's death ended the reign of the Egyptian monarchs and allowed Roman emperors to rule her land instead. She was the last pharaoh. To terminate the Ptolemy dynasty, Octavian had Caesarion killed and turned Egypt into a Roman province. Cleopatra's remaining children were raised by Octavia in Rome, with her daughter Cleopatra Selene eventually marrying King Juba II of Mauretania.

Suggested Readings

Cleopatra of Egypt: From History to Myth. Susan Walker and Peter Higgs, eds. (2001).

6
Chapter

The Roman Republic

Tiberius Gracchus and Gaius Gracchus

The brothers Tiberius Gracchus and Gaius Gracchus were reform-minded noblemen who propounded a series of popular reforms with the objective of reinvigorating both the strength of the Roman army and the morale of the citizenship. Though they attracted considerable support among commoners, they alienated the powerful landowning nobility, and both eventually were murdered. Their deaths marked the beginning of an era of growing political violence that contributed to the collapse of the Roman Republic. What basic problems did the Gracchi perceive in the society of late republican Rome and what solutions did they propose?

* * *

The end of the Punic Wars in 146 BCE left Rome in control of an extensive Mediterranean empire. Among the new provinces were many with considerable resources, ripe for exploitation and new peoples whose taxes could further enrich Roman civilization. The long Punic wars had set in motion considerable social and political changes, although the consequences were not immediately discernible. Roman military successes, together with newly acquired wealth, fed a new mood of arrogance and materialism, which undermined the civic virtue that had long been republican Rome's pride. Agricultural concepts adopted from conquered Carthage and Greece, where large plantations had been the rule, slowly supplanted the traditional Roman emphasis on the small independent farm. Rome's senatorial class, its wealth boosted by imperial riches and slaves, increasingly dominated the countryside, investing in large farms of *latifundia* that were worked by slaves. Small farmers, already under pressure from these developments, were further burdened by the military service requirements. Those who could no longer make a living by farming often abandoned the countryside for the cities, where they were absorbed into a growing mob of the impoverished and unemployed. Ultimately, the mob's potential for violent and disruptive riots compelled a government policy of "bread and circuses" to distract the lower classes. Roman society was, by the middle of the second century BCE, increasingly unstable, marked by a growing disparity between rich and poor and weakened by the erosion of civic virtue.

Tiberius Gracchus was not the first to recognize the need to address Rome's many social, economic and political problems; he was, however, the first soldier-statesman to propose serious and comprehensive remedies. Tiberius Sempronius Gracchus was a member of a distinguished family. Scipio Africanus the Elder, the conqueror of Hannibal, was his grandfather. His father, who shared his name, was an accomplished statesman and soldier, while his mother Cornelia, Scipio's daughter, was known as a highly cultured woman. Tiberius entered public life early, serving as an augur, or interpreter of omens at age ten, before serving under his brother-in-law Aemilianus at the siege of Carthage in 146 BCE. Tiberius took as his wife Claudia, the daughter of an important government official. By 137 BCE, he was serving as quaestor, or financial administrator, to the army of Gaius Hostilius Mancinus in Spain. There, while traveling through Etruria, he observed that the large estates worked by slaves crowded out independent farmers. While in Spain, Tiberius enhanced his diplomatic reputation when he negotiated free passage for a Roman army of 20,000 defeated by the Numantines.

It was upon his return from Spain that Tiberius began to champion the cause of reform and the common people. His interest in these issues likely stemmed from his familiarity with Greek political theory, a slave rebellion in Sicily and the increasingly inequitable conditions he perceived in Rome. Elected as a tribune in 133 BCE, Tiberius won the support of an influential group of senators for reforms that might restore social stability, economic prosperity and perhaps civic virtue. Despite the opposition of resentful nobles led by his cousin Scipio Africanus the Younger, Tiberius succeeded in gaining passage of a law that provided for a more equitable distribution of land among small farmers. His decision to submit the measure first to the Popular Assembly, however, contravened accepted political protocol and bruised some Senatorial egos, perhaps costing him needed support in that body and arousing suspicions about the popular young tribune's efforts to mobilize popular opinion behind his efforts.

The consequences of such suspicions became evident that summer when Tiberius decided to seek a second term as tribune. Such a move was not illegal, but had previously occurred some two centuries earlier when the function of the tribunate was considerably different. Though Tiberius may have undertaken the unusual step in hopes of protecting his land reform bill, his opponents saw it as a sign of dangerous ambition. When Tiberius and his supporters gathered at the Assembly's meeting place to discuss his eligibility, fighting broke out for reasons that remain unclear and the tribune fled. A furious debate over Tiberius's intentions disrupted the Senate, which broke up as the supreme head of that body, P. Scipio Nasica, gathered those senators who agreed that Tiberius aspired to be dictator. These men, joined by others who opposed the reformist tribune, stormed the meeting place of the Assembly and assaulted a group of Tiberius's supporters. Some three hundred were clubbed and stoned to death; Tiberius Gracchus was murdered at the door of the Temple of Jupiter. All the bodies were thrown into the Tiber River.

The murder of Tiberius Gracchus marked the end of some four centuries of civil peace in Rome; political violence was to become increasingly endemic in future years. Tiberius arguably acted irresponsibly in his apparent effort to shift the balance of governing authority to the Popular Assembly and his opponents in the Senate and elsewhere wasted little time in authorizing the punishment or exile of the remaining Gracchans. There was no effort, however, to interfere with the recently enacted land legislation. Gaius Gracchus, meanwhile, was serving with the Roman army in Spain. Like his brother, he was appointed quaestor in 126 BCE and saw service in Sardinia, where a rebellion was underway. The Roman Senate, wary of the political repercussions of allowing another Gracchus into the capital, sought to keep Gaius distant by extending his quaestorship. Nonetheless, he returned in 123 BCE, again following in his brother's path by winning election as a tribune.

As a tribune, Gaius dedicated his energies to a broad range of reforms, including efforts to strengthen the popular voice in government. He proposed that any magistrate or tribune deposed by the Popular Assembly be barred from holding future office; hopefully, this would act as a brake on Senate influence over tribunes. Strengthening the political power of the equestrian (or wealthy middle) class to balance that of the nobility was another initiative that Gaius pursued. He also succeeded in passing a bill that prohibited courts authorized to impose the death penalty unless the Popular Assembly established them. Economic reforms were also among Gaius's concerns. In addition to reviving his brother's land reforms, Gaius won legislation that established colonies in southern Italy, where landless farmers could be settled. He also supported programs for road construction and repair throughout Italy, which brought employment and facilitated the development of the peninsula's resources. Additional legislation committed the state to buy and store grain with an eye to alleviating shortfalls and permitting citizens to purchase a grain ration at a considerably reduced price.

Such reforms were bound to draw opposition. Though Gaius won a second term as tribune with little controversy, those threatened by the reforms proved willing and capable of mobilizing against him. One strategy was to have another tribune introduce a program of agricultural and military reforms in the Senate in hopes of undercutting Gaius's support. Gaius responded with even more ambitious proposals of his own, including a colony to be founded on the site of Carthage to be settled by some 600 colonists with independent holdings. Opening more political issues, Gaius further proposed greater judicial duties for the Equites, the equestrian body, which further reduced the purvue of the Senate. He likewise proposed broadening the franchise to give all Latins full citizenship. These reforms proved too much for those who feared and resented Gaius's growing influence. While Gaius was absent, supervising the founding of his new colony, his enemies began spreading tales of his failures overseas, and the mob began to turn against him. On his return in 121 BCE, Gaius failed to gain reelection as a tribune even as a powerful opponent, Lucius Opimius, was elected consul. The latter quickly moved to mobilize the Senate, the Equites and the mob against the Gracchans. Having occupied the Aventine, the Gracchans were overcome and killed; some 3000 additional supporters of Gaius were later executed. Gaius fled across the Tiber, but his body was later found on a hill near the river. The Gracchi succeeded in introducing reforms that benefited the lower classes and temporarily alleviated some of Rome's economic difficulties. In the years to come, others sought to avenge the death of the Gracchi and realize their legacy. The long-term trends, however, were towards growing political violence, pandering to the mob and a succession of military men who sought to realize their own ambitions in politics. The foundations of Roman Republic were inexorably eroding, fatally undermined by the wealth generated by foreign conquest and the dissipation of the civic virtue so crucial to its existence.

Suggested Readings

Beard, Mary and Michael Crawford. *Rome in the Late Republic* (1985).

Scullard, H.H. *From the Gracchi to Nero* (1982).

Octavian

Octavian, later known as the emperor Augustus, was a military commander who played a central role in the political and military struggles following the assassination of Julius Caesar. Ultimately, he asserted his authority as the first emperor of Rome. His legacy is mixed, with his advocates crediting him for establishing political stability, prosperity and peace, which had eluded Rome in the last years of the Republic. His detractors describe him as a tyrant who was willing to resort to unscrupulous methods to assert his authority. What do you think?

* * *

Born Gaius Octavius in 63 BCE, the man who came to be known as Octavian was the grandnephew of Julius Caesar. His father died when he was still young and his mother raised him, though he quickly gained the favor of Caesar, who had him appointed to the College of Pontifices, a major priesthood, at age sixteen. Octavian was undergoing military training in Illyria when he learned of Caesar's assassination. His determination to avenge Caesar was strengthened when he discovered that he was named as chief heir to Caesar's estate. Returning to Rome, Octavian allied himself with Caesar's supporters and sought the friendship of Marc Antony, but Antony resented Caesar's preference of Octavian and likewise feared his ambition. For some months, military conflict, political uncertainty and Senate intrigues left Rome's future unclear. Antony's forces were defeated and he was driven across the Alps; Octavian emerged triumphant in Rome, where he was named consul at age twenty.

In 43 BCE, Octavian, in hopes of resolving the continuing crisis, met with Antony, and together with Antony's general Marcus Lepidus, agreed that they should jointly form the Second Triumvirate, a governing body with near dictatorial powers, empowered to dominate both Senate and state. The three divided the western provinces between them and planned a campaign against remaining republican forces and potential political opponents. Death warrants were issued and executed against 300 senators and 2000 knights; perhaps the most famous victim was the aged orator Cicero. His hands and head were displayed in the Forum, effective warning to those who opposed the triumvirate. With Lepidus governing Rome, Octavian and Antony next marched against Caesar's assassins, Brutus and Cassius. Following their defeat in Macedonia in 42 BCE, the two men committed suicide. By 40 BCE, the Second Triumvirate effectively controlled the Roman world, with Octavian given charge of the western provinces and Antony ruling the east. Lepidus was granted authority over Africa.

Inevitably, the ambitions of the triumvirs brought growing tensions. Octavian and Antony quarreled over control of Italy and were only temporarily reconciled when Octavian gave his sister as wife to Antony. One major remaining opponent of the Triumvirate, Sextus Pompeius, was finally defeated and executed in 36 BCE. In the aftermath of this victory, Octavian moved against Lepidus, who had sought to assert his control over Sicily. Abandoned by his own troops, Lepidus was compelled to submit to Octavian, who spared his life but deprived him of his authority. With the Second Triumvirate splintering, Octavian was emerging as the man capable of restoring order and peace. The public also saw in Octavian a defender of their cause and their traditions. Antony, in contrast, was perceived as too fond of the traditions and ways of the east.

The final phase in the collapse of the Second Triumvirate grew out of developments in Egypt, where Antony's infatuation with Cleopatra was to have unexpected and significant political repercussions. Bored with his wife, Octavian's sister, Antony sent her back to Rome and shortly afterwards married Cleopatra. This did much to diminish his stature among Romans. Following military campaigns aimed at extending his authority in east-central Asia, Antony returned to Alexandria, where in 34 BCE, he arranged a ceremony in which Cleopatra was declared Queen of Kings, to rule jointly over Egypt and Cyprus with her son Caesarion. Antony's assertion that Caesarion was the legitimate son of Julius Caesar was a challenge that Octavian could not overlook. Relations between the two remaining triumvirs deteriorated rapidly, making war inevitable. In 31 BCE, Octavian defeated the forces of Antony and Cleopatra in a naval engagement off Actium. Both Antony and Cleopatra committed suicide within the year and Caesarion was murdered on Octavian's order. The century of civil strife that had followed the deaths of the Gracchi was now over, but at the cost of the disintegration of the Republic.

Octavian returned to Rome in 29 BCE, now well positioned to assert unchallenged authority. The Roman people were weary of civil strife, political violence and war and were willing to exchange many of the liberties of the republic for the resolution of these ills. Like many authoritarian rulers in later ages, Octavian acquired unprecedented powers for himself while claiming to preserve traditional liberties. As of 30 BCE, he had possessed the power of a tribune, which gave him veto power over and control of the assemblies; this proved crucial to consolidating his authority in future years. The Senate also confirmed his ultimate authority over the provinces, which together with the powers of consul, a position he held thirteen times during his reign, gave him control not only of Rome and Italy, but also throughout the empire. Octavian also held the highest position of religious authority as Pontifex Maximus, a title he had gained after the death of Lepidus.

In 27 BCE, Octavian was given the name Augustus, a new and unique designation that connoted reverence, if not holiness. Though emperor in all but name, Augustus took care to avoid the appearance of establishing a monarchy. Indeed, he adopted the title of *princeps*, or "first citizen." He avoided displays of ostentation or arrogance, respected the dignity of the Senate, mingled easily with the common people and adopted a simple personal lifestyle. Yet the Principate, as the government came to be known, was not the reincarnation of the republic, as Augustus maintained. It was rather a benevolent monarchy, well administered with an eye to public relations and to avoiding any appearance of arbitrary power. Those institutions that were erected as bulwarks against dictatorship, the assemblies, were effectively co-opted under Augustus's disarming hand. Though there was now no means to successfully challenge the *princeps'* power, there was increasingly less desire or reason to do so. Augustus' defenders note that closer control over provincial government and greater efficiency had reduced official corruption and exploitation. Rome's new imperial bureaucracy, responsible now only to the *princeps*, afforded greater social mobility, as government service was open to all classes, with talent as a primary criterion. Augustus enhanced his popularity by presenting himself as a defender of traditional Roman virtues and by supporting the passage of sumptuary laws aimed at restricting displays of extravagance. Another body of laws sought to stabilize and encourage marriage. Aware of the traditional popular concern with the status of independent farmers, Augustus also approved legislation to restore agriculture in Italy.

A second dimension of Augustus's reign involved cultural and intellectual attainments. Referred to as the "Augustan Age," this era brought renewed optimism, patriotism and creative accomplishments in both history and literature. Augustus was a patron of the historian Livy, who dedicated himself to writing a monumental history of Rome stressing the eternal quality of roman virtues. The poets Horace and Ovid did much to establish Rome's literary supremacy during this era. Virgil's epic poem *Aeneid* was perhaps the greatest manifestation of the new spirit reflected in culture. Some even saw in Virgil's hero Aeneas a reflection of Augustus, the personification of hope, justice and peace. Roman architecture, incorporating Greek elements in a distinctly Roman style, further affirmed Rome's cultural vitality.

Augustus, though married three times, left no sons as heir. His stepson and son-in-law Tiberius succeeded him when he died in August 14 CE at age seventy-six. Tiberius initially proved an adept ruler, maintaining the new imperial structure that Augustus had erected, but even during his reign the potential dangers inherent in the system became evident. Increasingly unpopular and suspicious in his later years, Tiberius resorted to harsh measures to suppress opponents and died in 37 CE with no public honors and little public grief. He was succeeded by Gaius, son of Germanicus and Agrippina, known to history as Caligula. His excesses and cruelties demonstrated that, in the wrong hands, the accumulated powers of the emperor could prove disastrous.

Suggested Readings

Scullard, H.H. *From the Gracchi to Nero* (1981).
Wells, Colin. *The Roman Empire* (1984).

7

Chapter

The Roman Empire: Religious Change and Adaptation: Paul and Constantine

Paul of Tarsus

Paul of Tarsus (born 'Saul') is one of the central figures in the early history of Christianity, which would emerge as the dominant religion in Europe in the first millennium CE. What do Paul's experiences reveal about Jewish and Christian interaction in the early history of the new religion? How did the conditions of the Roman Empire both facilitate and impede the spread of the Christian message(s)?

* * *

Paul occupies a particularly prominent position in the development of Christian doctrine in the 1st century CE, and he may even be the key figure in the earliest history of the religion. However, the details of his life can only be discerned from the Christians' own documents, including the writings attributed to him, constituting a large portion of today's Christian New Testament. Nevertheless, as at least some of these writings date to the 50s CE, and since most scholars agree that the four canonical Gospels (Matthew, Mark, Luke, John) were probably composed decades later, they are probably the earliest texts to have arisen from the movement. Thus, if analyzed for their historical, rather than their strictly theological content, these texts can be particularly helpful in reconstructing the controversies and challenges faced by the Christians at their formative stage.

The main biographical elements of Paul's life are contained in the 'Acts of the Apostles', a work that should probably be credited to the same author as the Gospel According to 'Luke'. [As is the case of the books attributed to Paul, it was common practice in ancient times to attribute a book to an authoritative figure, even if it was actually composed by some other writer.] Paul was born in Tarsus, the capital city of Cilicia, a Roman province in what is today southern Turkey. However, his original name was 'Saul', and he possessed a unique heritage and identity, within his city and the Roman Empire as a whole. Saul claims to have been born a Roman citizen, which would suggest that his parents, or some earlier ancestor, had been accorded this signal privilege at some point. Roman citizenship was a very rare commodity outside the Italian peninsula at the time, but the documents do not explain at what point Saul's family had received it. He seems to have come from a family of tentmakers, and, at various points along his missionary journeys, Saul used his training in this craft to supplement his income.

Despite his connections to the Romans who dominated the Empire at this time, Saul also proclaimed himself a Jew, and one who had traveled to Jerusalem to study Jewish traditions under a famous teacher called Gamaliel. Saul specifically attached himself to the group of Jewish intellectuals and religious officials called 'Pharisees', who are familiar both from the Christian accounts of the life of Jesus and from later Jewish tradition. It was as a member of the temple police, and as an enforcer of Jewish religious policy, that Saul claims first to have encountered a new religious sect, growing up around the followers of Jesus of Nazareth, who had been crucified under Roman authority in the early 30s CE.

Saul later claimed that he had been active in persecuting these followers of Jesus, but then, while on a journey to Damascus, he had been temporarily blinded and converted to belief in the Christian message. From this point, he proclaimed that Jesus was the Messiah who had been promised to the Jews, and his name was changed to 'Paul', to symbolize his rejection of his previous opinion regarding Jesus' identity. Nevertheless, very soon after he began his 'mission' of spreading what he considered the 'evangelion'—or 'good news' in Greek—of the resurrection of Jesus, Paul was embroiled in controversy with some of the other followers of Jesus. The most prominent of these Jewish Christians was Peter, one of the 12 original 'disciples' mentioned in the Gospel accounts.

By the late 40s CE, Paul seems to have been arguing to his co-religionists that the Christian message should be spread to non-Jews (called 'Gentiles' in Jewish tradition), as well as to the Jews themselves. After a bitterly contentious conference in Jerusalem on the issue, Peter and Paul seem to have parted ways, taking with them the adherents to their positions. Paul would continue to insist, over the protests of others, that converts to Christianity need not be 'circumcised', as a visual marker of an assumed Jewish identity, and he would also inject baldly anti-Jewish language into his writings—arguing that the Jews had once been the 'chosen people', but were no longer. The centuries of Christian hatred and persecution of Jews stemmed, in part, from this decision to separate the Christian religion from the Jewish traditions and practices from which it had originally sprung.

Further controversies arose wherever Paul spread his message, which he began to do even more energetically, throughout the Greek mainland and Asia Minor over the following decade. For examples, he was asked his opinion regarding the eating of food sacrificed to non-Christian gods, the proper role of women in Christian worship and households, how to reconcile sexuality with Christian ethics, and how Christians should live their lives in communities that did not adhere to their views. His answers formed the basis for the earliest Christian 'theology', or 'study of God', but it is perhaps more interesting to reflect on the sorts of questions that arose. Given the difficulties of travel in the Mediterranean—even at a time of unusual peace and safety, such as the 1st century—it was only natural that different communities of Christians soon had very different ideas about even the most fundamental Christian doctrines. Paul used his 'Epistles' as a means of enforcing religious 'orthodoxy' ('correct belief')—but the Christians would continue, for many centuries, to struggle to define what, precisely, they believed about certain key issues.

Christian texts suggest that Paul was beaten, imprisoned, and ultimately sent to Rome to stand trial before the Emperor. As a Roman citizen, Paul claimed the privilege to have his case heard directly by the ultimate arbiter of justice in the Empire, and the most reliable accounts end with his awaiting trial in Rome, still writing and/or dictating his messages to the Christian communities in various cities. Later legends maintain that he was executed, in a general persecution of Christians launched by the Emperor Nero as a reaction to the Great Fire of Rome in 64.

Suggested Reading:

A. N. Wilson, Paul: *The Mind of the Apostle,* New York: W.W. Norton, 1997.

Constantine

The first Roman emperor to convert to Christianity, Constantine the Great established freedom of worship for his co-religionists. In 313 CE, Constantine issued the Edict of Milan, which ended the intolerance of Diocletian and afforded Jews and Christians religious freedom. He ruled the Roman Empire from Constantinople, which became the new capital of his vast realm. At the midpoint of his reign (312–337 CE), Constantine headed the Church's first great ecumenical council, which sought to resolve disputes among Christians. How did Constantine's acceptance of Christianity influence the Roman Empire? How unique was his tolerant attitude regarding religious beliefs?

* * *

Flavius Valerius Constantinus (Constantine) was born sometime between 274 CE and 288 CE at Naissa, to Constantinus Chlorus, a Roman officer, and St. Helena, a woman of humble origins but considerable abilities. To rule the vast Roman empire, Diocletian, shortly after being named emperor in 284 CE, selected Maximian to share that title, and in 293 CE, named Constantius I and Galerius as Caesars, or junior emperors, in effect. For a period, Galerius demanded that Constantine remain at his court. In 305 CE, both Diocletian and Maximian relinquished power. Constantinus now became known as Augustus and ruled in the new West. Constantinus's reign proved peaceful and prosperous in Gaul, Britain, and Spain, while instability beset the East. Nevertheless, Constantinus prepared to move against the Picts, found north of Hadrian's Wall in the area the Romans called Caledonia (later Scotland), and sought to have Constantine help lead the Roman army. Due to Constantine's popularity with the legions, Galerius was reluctant to accede to that request, fearing that he might lose control of the army. Having received grudging permission to depart, Constantine, along with a few compatriots, left quickly, taking off on horseback. They reached the French coast before Galerius was able to change his mind. In 306 CE, the gravelly ill Constantinus perished at York, followed by the decision of his troops to salute Constantine as emperor of Britain. An angered Galerius was possibly placated to some extent when Constantine informed him that the idea had been concocted by the soldiers. Relenting, Galerius allowed Constantine to receive the title of Caesar and chose Severus II to serve as Augustus in the West.

Soon, Galerius confronted another threat to his supremacy when a revolt occurred in Italy, spurred by high taxes and Rome's loss of the tax exemption it had long enjoyed. Maxentius, the son of Maximianus, was proclaimed emperor, and soon urged his father to abandon his retirement and serve as co-emperor. Constantine, for his part, began claiming the title of Augustus, undoubtedly emboldened by his possession of the most loyal army in the empire. Severus II was sent by Galerus to quell the disturbance in Italy but was bested in battle and executed. Concerned that anarchy and civil war might reappear, Diocletian agreed to head a peace conference in Camuntum, along the Danube River. The resulting compact brought about Constantine's demotion to Caesar and Valerius Licinianus Licinius's appointment as the western Augustus. Maximianus was compelled to abdicate and his son was denounced as an enemy of the people.

Initially, Constantine avoided becoming ensnared in the royal struggles, even acceding to his demotion. However, in 311 CE, following the death of Galerius and condemnations of Constantine by Maxentius, war broke out. Maxentius boasted a far larger army, but Constantine readily marched into Italy, where he crushed a strong military force near Turin. After triumphing in Verona, Constantine headed for Rome. As he prepared to meet Maxentius's far larger army in October 312 CE, Constantine was emboldened by a vision he had assuring him of victory if he fought under the sign of the cross. Another story had Constantine demanding that the shields of his soldiers be emblazoned with the Greek letters *chi* and *rho*, representing the initial letters of Christ's name. Constantine, who had aligned with Licinius, defeated Maxentius's forces at the battle of the Milvian Bridge, where their leader was killed. Avoiding vengeful treatment, Constantine carried out no executions of his defeated foes.

Now, Licinius, who had come to rule in the east, and Constantine stood as the twin emperors of the sprawling empire. In 313 CE, the two gathered in Milan where they delivered a proclamation allowing for freedom of worship for all religious groups. In addition, Constantine declared the Christian church to be a legal body entitled to possess property, and ordered the return of property that had been taken from Christians. The partnership between Constantine and Licinius—both ambitious, strong-willed individuals—proved increasingly difficult, with warfare occurring in 314 CE, followed by an uneasy peace. Each sought to place his son or sons in a position of power, with Lininius declaring Licinius Caesar, and Constantine doing the same with Crispus and Constantine II. In July 324 CE, their two massive armies—purportedly containing more than 100,000 infantrymen apiece— met at Adrianople, ending with Licinius's defeat at Hadrianopolis and Chrysopolis. Initially, Constantine spared the lives of Licinius and Licinius II but when they began plotting against him, the Roman Senate ordered their executions.

Standing as the undisputed ruler of the Roman Empire, Constantine initiated the reconstruction of the old Greek city of Byzantium, which would be renamed Constantinopole and serve as the capital of the East. He concentrated on ensuring the viability of the empire, attending to political, economic, and religious matters. His nephews, Dalmatius and Hanninbalianus ruled over lesser provinces, while his sons Constantius, Constantien, and Constans were named his successors. In 325 CE, Constantine presided over the Council of Nicaea, where bishops from throughout the empire gathered to explore religious questions. They agreed on the doctrine of the Holy Trinity, claiming that God was represented by the Father, the Son, and the Holy Ghost. The bishops condemned the Arian heresy, which declared Jesus to be a lesser figure.

Tragedy struck Constantine's house when his wife Fausta wrongly accused Crispus, his son by an earlier marriage, of committing adultery with her and seeking to take the throne. An angered Constantine ordered the death of Crispus, but subsequently had Fausta executed as well.

In his final days, Constantine prepared to go into battle once more, this time against the Persian king Shapur. But prior to that encounter, he died at Nicomedia on May 22, 337 CE, having been baptized at the end of his life. The Eastern Orthodox church came to regard Constantine as a saint.

Suggested Readings

Grant, Michael. *Constantine the Great: The Man and His Times* (1994).

8

Chapter

Empire Builders
in the Middle Ages

Frederick I, Barbarossa

Frederick I Barbarossa, Holy Roman emperor and German king, assumed the throne following an era in which the unity of the German empire and the authority of the emperor had eroded following disputes with the papacy and civil war. Among Frederick's chief concerns were a revival of imperial authority and a reorganization of the empire on a new and stronger basis. How did Frederick seek to accomplish these objectives and how successful was he in strengthening the new Hohenstaufen Empire?

* * *

Frederick Barbarossa was born in Waiblingen in or about 1123, the son of Frederick II of Hohenstaufen, Duke of Swabia, and Judith, a Welf princess from Bavaria. His later elevation as German ruler came in large part due to the decision of Conrad III, then the German king, not to promote his own infant son, whose succession would have opened a long and potentially dangerous period of minority rule; rather he chose his nephew, Frederick, whose abilities were already evident at the time. Frederick came to young adulthood in the aftermath of the Investiture Conflict of the late eleventh and early twelfth century. That contest had pitted Pope Gregory VII against the German Emperor Henry IV in a quarrel over whether the pope or the emperor had the authority to invest, or appoint higher clergy. Traditionally, the emperor held the authority to present the land that went with a given church office. Gregory's denial of this authority opened up fundamental issues of temporal authority and brought chaos to Germany when the pope excommunicated Henry. Henry was ultimately compelled to seek to have the excommunication lifted, an action that seemed to acknowledge the emperor's subordination to the church.

Nonetheless, Germany was wracked by civil war from 1077 until 1122, a period during which the princes sought to loosen imperial bonds to serve their own purposes. Though the Concordat of Worms (1122) ended the conflict with a compromise of the investiture issue, the political relationships in Germany were drastically altered, with imperial authority greatly reduced and the power of the princes enhanced. Likewise in northern Italy, many of the Italian communes gained considerable autonomy from the now-weakened empire.

Accordingly, when Frederick, then Duke of Swabia, was elected as German king in 1152, any ambitions he might have had for consolidating his authority in Germany, and perhaps even being crowned emperor, were contingent on his ability to reestablish the authority of the monarchy. As the old imperial system had been effectively destroyed in the course of the Investiture Controversy, Frederick was faced with the fundamental task of reorganizing power relationships in the German empire. This would require reconciling the German princes, dealing with a papacy that always jealousy guarded its prerogatives, and reasserting German authority over the not-always-dependable Italian communes.

Frederick benefited from the broad desire among German princes for a restoration of order following long decades of conflict. It was generally believed that Frederick, who represented the union of two important families, the Welfs and the Staufers, might be capable of bringing peace to Germany. Known for his determination and astuteness, Frederick was also physically impressive, gaining his nickname from his red beard; one story holds that it was in Italy that the name "Barbarossa" was first commonly heard during the course of one of Frederick's visits. As a first step towards the restoration of monarchical authority in Germany, Frederick had to assess the base of his power there. Hohenstaufen holdings were concentrated in Swabia in the southwest corner of the kingdom; Frederick lacked the scattered territorial holdings that had given earlier kings an advantage. Here, his marriage to Beatrice, the Duchess of Burgundy in 1156, brought new opportunities, as Frederick could now claim authority in both Burgundy and Provence. By combining these territories with Lombardy, in northern Italy, Frederick created a central stronghold of Hohenstaufen authority from which he could assert his power in Saxony, Bavaria and Tuscany in central Italy.

In Germany as elsewhere, one of Frederick's major objectives was to revive monarchical power by reimposing a feudal system, which required that the princes accept royal authority. To win the cooperation of these powerful nobles, Frederick bequeathed considerable privileges, which accorded the great princes considerable autonomy at the local level. Once they were reconciled to his rejuvenated system of feudal relationships, and accepted their subordination to the king, these same princes were useful instruments of control over the lesser nobility. In some cases, Frederick sought to ensure his own domination by pitting powerful princes against one another. In 1156, for example, he created the duchy of Austria as a counterbalance to the power of the Bavarian ruler Henry the Lion. In later years, when Henry proved an undependable ally in the Frederick's campaigns to subjugate the Italian communes and balked at submitting to a royal court, he was deprived of his territorial possessions. Henry's fall from power provided the opportunity for a further restructuring of the German lands in 1180. Saxony was divided into two lesser duchies; Bavaria was granted to Frederick's loyal supporter Otto of Wittelsbach, whose accession marked the beginning of a dynasty that endured until 1918. Through these actions and by further parceling out territories to loyal bishops and princes, Frederick reduced the larger vassal states to relatively insignificant territories that could be more easily controlled. In his own directly ruled possessions, Frederick pursued a policy of administrative centralization, creating new non-feudal structures. In those areas too far afield for the direct exercise of royal authority, Frederick relied on loyal princes to serve his needs. In general, Frederick proved adept at utilizing a variety of schemes to reimpose royal authority across Germany.

Historically, the German king had the right to claim the crown of the "Holy Empire," a term that Frederick frequently employed (it would not become officially the Holy Roman Empire until 1254, though for the sake of convenience, the name is often employed at earlier dates). In 1154, Frederick accompanied his army to Italy, where his efforts to compel the submission of the north Italian communes and the more troublesome city of Milan brought little immediate success, though he was granted the Lombard crown at Pavia. The following year, Pope Adrian IV bestowed the crown of the Holy Roman Emperor on the German king, but relations with the Italian communes and the papacy soon deteriorated. Frederick had antagonized Roman representatives in 1155 when he refused their demand for five thousand pounds of gold in return for the imperial crown, insisting that his empire had superseded that of Rome. The next year, the pope provoked Frederick when he insisted that Frederick held his lands only as a fief from the pope. Frederick could not accept the implication that he was a vassal of the pope. Once again, a Holy Roman Emperor found himself facing a dispute over the boundaries of papal authority.

Through both diplomacy and warfare, Frederick extended his authority into northern Italy, but his tenuous claim to authority there was broken when Italians rebelled against the heavy-handed rule of German imperial officials. By 1158, Milan, Placenza, Brescia and Cremona were among the cities protesting the loss of their communal liberties to imperial governors. This event marked the beginning of lengthy though intermittent warfare between the Italian cities and imperial forces that lasted until 1183. As Frederick's armies battled in Italy, the papacy was inevitably drawn into the conflict, and the new pope Alexander III sought to bring together an anti-imperial alliance. Frederick's successful capture of Milan in 1162 only temporarily improved his fortunes, as most of the cities now joined the pope to create the Lombard League. Frederick countered by supporting a succession of anti-popes, thus recapitulating a feature of earlier struggles between secular rulers and the papacy during the Investiture Conflict. Defeated at Legano in 1176, Frederick was left no choice but to compromise. In 1176, he acknowledged Alexander II as pope and in 1183 agreed to the Peace of Constance, which granted Lombard demands for autonomy, but recognized Frederick's largely nominal imperial authority over the Italian cities.

Frederick failed to impose on the Italians the degree of imperial authority that he desired, but the long conflict ended with Lombardy accepting the emperor's distant authority; likewise, the breach with the papacy was at least temporarily resolved. The long campaign had produced troubles within Germany, most notably with Henry the Lion, but Frederick successfully resolved those problems in the 1180s. Having rebuilt a badly weakened Germany and successfully claimed the imperial crown, Frederick was a figure of considerable stature in the last decades of the twelfth century. His legendary status was assured when in 1189, together with three other major European monarchs, he led the Third Crusade, by which Christian Europe hoped to recapture Jerusalem from Muslim control. Leading an army overland through Hungary and Bulgaria, Frederick arrived in the Byzantine Empire. There, in June 1190, he was drowned while crossing the Calycadnus River in what is now Turkey. The Hohenstaufen Empire was plunged into crisis in the decades following his death and the imperial authority that Frederick worked so tirelessly to establish once again devolved to the princes; Germany remained fragmented for centuries to come.

Suggested Readings

Barraclough, Geoffrey. *The Origins of Modern Germany* (1984).
Fuhrmann, Horst. *Germany in the High Middle Ages* (1986).

Saladin

Saladin, or Salah al-Din Yusuf bin Ayub, was a twelfth century Muslim military leader and the first Ayyubid sultan of Egypt. His accomplishments were numerous, as he brought colleges and hospitals to Cairo, revitalized the Egyptian economy, and devoted considerable effort to the reorganization of military forces that would later assure his fame. Saladin is best known, however, for his part in the Third Crusade, during which he played a major role in recapturing Jerusalem for Islam after an eighty-nine-year-long Christian occupation. He was greatly respected not only by fellow Muslims, but also by Europeans contemporaries. Why was it that, in an age of religious warfare, Saladin was so widely respected in both the Christian and Muslim worlds?

* * *

Saladin was born in 1138 in the Mesopotamian village of Tikrit, now in Iraq. An Armenian Kurd whose Arabic name translates as "righteousness of the faith," Saladin moved to Damascus at age eight, in the company of his father Ayyub and his uncle Shirkuh, both of whom had served the Saracen warrior-chief Zengi. Saladin spent ten years in Damascus, during which time he devoted considerable study to the Qur'an, enhancing his understanding of the Sunni Muslim faith. In 1152, he entered into the service of the Syrian ruler Nur al-Din, the son of Zengi. He was soon granted his own fief and undertook what was to become and lengthy and illustrious military career. By 1156, he won appointment as deputy to Shirkuh, who served Nur al-Din as military governor of Damascus.

Though Saladin had established a respectable place in society, his success came despite the disadvantages of his birth. As an ethnic Kurd, both Turks and Arabs looked him upon with some degree of disdain. Though he had largely surmounted this obstacle by the time he reached young adulthood, avenues to significant advancement might have been restricted had it not been for the particular circumstances of the period. By the late twelfth century, the Islamic world remained politically fragmented; the Seljuk Turk empire had, since the previous century, been increasingly subdivided. Antagonistic caliphs (religious leaders) in Baghdad and Cairo compounded the disunity of the Muslim world. The Christian kingdom in Jerusalem, which many Muslims saw as both a threat and a challenge, continued to exist in the midst of Islam largely because of the absence of unity amongst the Muslim peoples. Zengi had been among the first to advocate a new holy war, or *jihad*, at about the time of Saladin's birth. Saladin's great fortune was to come of age at the very time when a movement for Muslim unity was gradually building, with the ultimate expectation of driving the Christians from Jerusalem.

Saladin's path to renown began in 1167, when he accompanied Shirkuh and a Syrian army to Egypt, which was by that time a periodic battleground between the Seljuk Turks and the Crusaders. Nur al-Din had concluded that Egypt threatened the tenuous unity of his empire, as the Fatimid rulers of Egypt, and especially the vizier Shawar, had proven incompetent and untrustworthy, occasionally allying with the Crusaders. Shawar would be of little value in opposing the armies of Al-maric, the King of Jerusalem, whose proximity was worrisome. Furthermore, the un-orthodox caliph of Cairo posed a threat to Sunni conformity. Saladin was thus drawn into a lengthy and complicated series of military expeditions into Egypt, where "Saracens," as the Christians often referred to any Muslim forces, fought Cru-saders. By 1169, Shawar had been assassinated and Shirkuh installed as the new vizier, with Saladin serving as his deputy. Shirkuh's death three months later gave Saladin command of the Syrian army and the post of vizier, with the title of "the con-quering prince" bestowed by the now compliant caliph. The caliph's death in 1171 made Saladin the undisputed ruler of Egypt, but he governed with a moderate hand, refusing to seize the wealth of the Fatimids or endorse punitive measures against for-mer enemies. He did, however, eject the Fatimids from their palaces and opened the gated city of Cairo to the common people. His reconstruction of Cairo included the building of needed fortresses like the Citadel, but also hospitals and schools. Be-cause of his attention to the needs of common Egyptians, Muslim and Christian alike, Saladin soon built a reputation as a benevolent ruler. The pacification of Egypt, complete by 1174, proved to be only the first step towards realizing Saladin's greater ambitions.

Though Saladin had done much to strengthen the Seljuk Empire, Nur al-Din grew increasingly suspicious about the ultimate designs of his subordinate. Saladin, during the years in which he consolidated his authority in Egypt, had seemed frus-tratingly hesitant to expand the war against the Christians. On the other hand, Nur al-Din's jealousy of his increasingly famous lieutenant was a cause of concern for Sal-adin. When Nur al-Din died in 1174, Saladin accepted the succession of his eleven year-old son Malikas es-Salih largely because it would have been unseemly to chal-lenge his authority so soon after his father's death. Later the same year, however, Sal-adin embarked for Syria, ostensibly for the purpose of supporting es-Salih against some rebelling chieftains. More probably, Saladin perceived an opportunity to win control of the empire for himself. The conquest of Syria, begun in 1174, with the ul-timate objective of unifying Muslims under a single leader, was the second major un-dertaking of Saladin's career. During the following twelve years, Saladin successfully asserted his authority in Damascus, Aleppo, Mosul and over most of Iraq.

By compelling the subordination and allegiance of the rulers of numerous towns and provinces, Saladin gradually isolated the Latin kingdom of Jerusalem, though he observed an uneasy peace with the Christians into the late 1180s. In 1187, the tenuous truce broke down. Reginald of Chatillon, the commander of the fortress town of el-Kerak, which sat astride an important trade route between Egypt and Mecca, had been increasingly provocative towards passing Arab caravans. When he seized an especially rich caravan, Saladin responded with a call for *jihad* against the Christians. The battle of Hattin ended with victory for Arab forces and the execution of the defeated Reginald. Saladin's army now marched on Jerusalem, which was under siege by September 1187. Marshaling knights, archers and siege machines, Saladin oversaw an assault that culminated in early October with the breaching of the city's walls. Surviving Christians were allowed to leave the city on payment of a ransom. It was a considerable contrast to the Christian capture of the city in 1099, which had been accompanied by the unrestrained slaughter of Muslims.

Saladin's capture of the Holy City for Islam ensured his lasting fame in the Muslim world. It also provoked the Third Crusade, which began in 1189. Saladin failed to capture the small but important Christian kingdom of Tyre, which left the Crusaders a base in the region. The Third Crusade drew Richard Lionheart, Philip of France and the Frederick Barbarossa into the effort to recapture Jerusalem for Christianity. Though Philip's efforts to take Acre in 1191 failed, Richard proved more successful, destroying the city's walls with catapults. Saladin was unable to relieve the city and Crusader forces seized it. Richard's legendary sense of chivalry failed him here, for when negotiations over prisoner exchange dragged on, Richard ordered the execution of some 2700 Muslim captives. Though Philip, faced with challenges to his rule, returned to France, Richard marched his forces down the coast to Jaffa. The following year brought four campaigns in Palestine, with Richard's forces generally besting those of Saladin. The Muslim leader was compelled to resort to a scorched-earth policy, even poisoning the wells of Jerusalem when the city seemed threatened. Saladin's fortunes improved when Richard grew weary of the conflict, fearing that even if he gained Jerusalem, it might prove indefensible. In September 1192, Richard agreed to a treaty that left only a small strip of coast to the Latin kingdom, though passage to Jerusalem for Christians was guaranteed. Saladin returned to Damascus, where he died in 1193 following an illness.

Saladin's accomplishment, the unification of the Muslim world and the capture of Jerusalem, ensured his fame among Muslims. But his greater accomplishment was to win the praise of many non-Muslims, Christians and Europeans for his courage, generosity of spirit and military leadership. In an era in which chivalric values were highly esteemed in Europe, Saladin's reputation was assured.

Suggested Reading

Lane-Poole, Stanley. *Saladin and the Fall of Jerusalem* (1898, 2003).
Reston, James, Jr. *Warriors of God: Richard the Lionheart and Saladin in the Third Crusade* (2001).

9 Chapter

Medieval Thought

Peter Abelard and Héloïse

Abelard and Heloise loved, lost, and then found a new form of love in 12th-century France, but their story is no merely romantic saga. They may have been the foremost intellectuals of their time, and their critical spirit and reliance on human reason disturbed the highest echelons of power in their society. What do their experiences reveal about the battle of faith and reason in the Middle Ages? What do their lives, together and apart, reveal about the status of women in the period?

* * *

A joint biography of Abelard and Héloïse is certainly appropriate; theirs was a passionate and erotic relationship as well as a meeting of minds. The main sources of information for their lives are Abelard's own account of his 'calamities', written in 1132-3, and an extensive set of letters exchanged between the two. Everything attests to the intellectual excitement of the era, when old assumptions were being subjected to rigorous analysis and traditional boundaries were being stretched to accommodate new ideas.

Abelard was born to a minor noble in Brittany in northwestern France, and he quickly demonstrated an aptitude for learning. In his adolescence and early adulthood, Abelard wandered from one cathedral school to another, looking for a 'master' who was worthy to be his teacher. In this era, schools were housed in and controlled by the Church, based at the cathedrals of bishops, and masters instructed young boys in the rudiments of grammar, logic, and rhetoric. This style of education did not encourage free thought or the creation of new ideas—masters recited concepts derived from the great thinkers of the Greco-Roman and early Christian past, and then students were expected to recite them back to the teacher and use them in 'disputation' with each other. Abelard soon tired of this limited sort of instruction, hoping to use his own formidable reasoning abilities to find answers for himself.

At each school, Abelard claims to have found lazy and limited masters who became jealous of his superior skills. Even in Paris, the intellectual center of his society, Abelard was disenchanted—and he decided to open his own school, at age 22. It is difficult for us to imagine the milieu into which Abelard had entered. Debates between scholars were followed with the eagerness attending prize fights or wrestling matches today, and Abelard developed a reputation for triumphing over his peers by means of his superior logic, eloquence, and creativity. He reached the height of his fame in 1115, when he was awarded a chair (a formal position) at the cathedral school of Notre Dame in Paris.

At this point, he accepted a commission from the Canon Fulbert to become a private tutor to Fulbert's young and talented niece Héloïse. Because she was female, Héloïse was barred from the educational institutions available to men, and Fulbert's efforts to secure her an education—from the best professor available—may reveal an enlightened attitude on his part. In spite of this trust, Abelard (rather cold-bloodedly) details how he came to seduce his student—her side of the relationship can only be determined from her later letters to Abelard—and then she discovered she was pregnant.

In secret, Héloïse gave birth to a son, whom his parents named 'Astrolabe', a scientific instrument used for ship navigation. Abelard claims that he proposed a secret marriage to Héloïse; it had to be secret, if he, officially a member of the institutional Church, were to maintain his position at the school. However, despite the shame of giving birth to a child outside marriage, Héloïse refused, arguing (at least so he says) that she did not wish to jeopardize *his* career. In any event, Héloïse withdrew to a convent and became a nun—essentially removing herself from the 'marriage market' to which most aristocratic young women were consigned at the time.

Fulbert was less easily appeased, however. Presumably determined to get to the root of the problem, Fulbert paid a group of men to rush into Abelard's room and castrate him. It should not be forgotten that this was the Middle Ages, and such a violent 'surgery' could easily have been lethal for Abelard. Nevertheless, Abelard survived the operation but, because of the attendant scandal, was forced to resign his position and withdraw to a monastery. But Abelard did not cease questioning and challenging people whom he considered his intellectual inferiors.

Determined to make the Trinity—one of the fundamental doctrines of Christian belief, and subjected to intense scrutiny since the earliest days of the religion—understandable to the students who still clamored to him for instruction, Abelard composed a book on the subject. Because he attempted to use reason and logic to explain this religious concept, Abelard was accused of heresy and forced to defend his ideas at a council at Soissons in 1121. Proclaiming that the God who created human reason could be explained by human reason, Abelard lost his case, and he was forced to burn his book with his own hands. Thereafter, he went from monastery to monastery; at each, he claims, the other monks hounded and belittled him (and even tried to poison him, in one particularly inhospitable house.)

In 1140, he was again prosecuted as a heretic, excommunicated by the Pope, and told to disavow his books. He sought refuge in the monastery in Cluny, and the excommunication was lifted. The ban on his books, however, stayed in place. He finally died in 1142, but Héloïse lived on until 1163. In their later years, the two had developed a remarkable correspondence, touching on their personal lives as well as on their intellectual opinions and discoveries. According to legend, the two are now buried together in Paris' Père-Lachaise Cemetery, and their gravesite is a pilgrimage point for lovers to this day.

Suggested Readings:

Constant J. Mews, *Abelard and Heloise,* Oxford: Oxford University Press, 2005. Betty Radice, trans., *The Letters of Abelard and Heloise,* revised ed. by Michael Clanchy, New York: Penguin, 2003.

Thomas Aquinas

One of the leading medieval philosophers and theologians, Thomas Aquinas was considered the most important figure associated with scholasticism. His major work, Summa Theologica, attempted to synthesize Christian thought, which Aquinas sought to meld with Aristotle's rationalist teachings. Faith and reason, Aquinas contended, did not conflict. Individuals, he suggested, were entitled to human rights that governments should not circumscribe. How did Aquinas represent the ideals of Scholasticism? How important were his concepts in the development of Western education?

* * *

He was born Thomas d'Aquino, in 1224 or 1225, at his father's castle, Roccasecea, in Neapolitan territory. His father was Count Landulf of Aquino, a member of a southern Italian family; his mother was Countess Theodora of Theate, who came from noble Norman stock. His family was related to the emperors Henry VI and Frederick II, and to monarchs of Aragon, Castile, and France. Purportedly a holy hermit predicted great things for him, declaring, "He will enter the Order of Friars Preachers, and so great will be his learning and sanctity that in his day no one will be found to equal him." Following the tradition of the day regarding noble lads, Aquinas was sent off at the age of five to receive his earliest formal instruction. He was placed in the care of the Benedictine monastery at Monte Cassino, where his uncle Sinibald served as abbot, a future his family envisioned for him. When a battle involving papal and royal troops unfolded in Monte Cassino in 1239, Aquinas was removed from the monastery and enrolled at the University of Naples, where Aristotelian philosophy was featured; that school of thought highlighted the systematic, deductive study of logic. In 1243 or 1244, he determined to become a Dominican friar, notwithstanding the opposition of his family. As he traveled to Rome, however, Aquinas was grabbed by his brothers who took him back to Roccasecea. Over the course of a year, his mother attempted to dissuade him from following the path he had chosen, but to no avail.

Eventually, he was permitted to return to his order in the summer of 1245. He went with Albertus, a renowned teacher of Scholasticism, to Paris to continue his studies and then accompanied his mentor to Cologne in 1248. He was ordained a priest in 1250. Assigned to teach at the Dominican house of studies in Paris, Aquinas delivered lectures on *The Four Books of Sentences*, by Italian theologian Peter Lombard, which synthesized theological issues of both a historical and contemporary (as of the mid twelfth century) cast. Despite political and religious tussles, Aquinas received his doctorate in theology from the University in Paris 1256, following a papal order that deserving mendicant friars should be allowed to obtain that degree. He was also named professor of philosophy at the university, and began writing his book, *Summa contra Gentiles*, challenging pagan perceptions of reality. In 1259, he was ordered to report to Rome to serve as adviser and lecturer for the papal court of Urban IV. In 1266, he began crafting his most famous study, *Summa Theologia*, in which he examined Christian theology, God, Christ, and man. He continued working on the text for the next seven years, but never completed this monumental work, which provided his exposition of natural law. *Summa Theologica* offers Aquinas's analysis of the five "proofs" of God's existence: an initial mover, a first step in a chain of causes, a wholly essential being, a completely perfect being, and a designer who is rational. Aquinas's God was also a beneficent actor: "Since God is entirely good, He would permit evil to exist in His works only if He were so good and omnipotent that He might bring forth good even from the evil. It therefore pertains to the infinite goodness of God that he permits evil to exist and from this brings forth good."

Drawing from Aristotle, Aquinas also articulated a system of ethics in which humankind seeks the highest end. Human actions proved worthy if undertaken to honor God, while nefarious deeds resulted from a failure to adhere to reason and divine moral law. Virtue was to be prized, Aquinas noted: " There are virtues disposing the will towards love of God and fellowman: charity, justice and the like. And there are virtues like moderation and courage which temper the emotions to serve the good of the willer himself, to which his will is inclined by nature." Fortunately, Christ, provided the pathway to God. Teacher and exemplar, Christ also forgave sins, allowed for reconciliation with God, and opened the gates of heaven. The sacraments enabled Christ's humanity to be delivered to man, infusing necessary grace into sensuous beings.

Aquinas returned to Paris in 1268 or 1269, and soon became embroiled in controversies involving the French philosopher Siger de Brabant and others who hearkened to the work of Averroes, the great Arabian philosopher who was an important interpreter of Aristotle. The Church began to view Averroes with increasing suspicion, in part because of his denial of personal immorality.

For centuries, Western thought had been greatly influenced by the philosophy of St. Augustine (354–430), who underscored humankind's absolute dependence on grace. The Averroists contended that philosophy required no revelation, thus threatening church doctrine. Aquinas sought to reconcile the Augustinian focus on spirituality with the Averroist insistence that knowledge could be derived from sensory experience. Insisting on the compatibility of the two notions, Aquinas declared that certain truths could only be known through revelation, while others could only be received through experience.

Aquinas's determination was still greater, as he sought to produce a philosophical synthesis that would incorporate the tenets of Aristotle and various classical thinkers, Augustine and other founders of the Church, Averroes and several Islamic sages, Jews like Maimonides, and earlier Scholastic scholars.

In 1272, Aquinas moved to Naples, a site he had selected where a new Dominican school would be established. Suffering from physical and mental exhaustion in December 1273, he ceased writing, although certain accounts indicate that a mystical experience led to that decision. In early 1274, acting at the behest of Pope Gregory X, he headed for the Council of Lyon, but became ill and died on March 7 at the Cistercian monastery in Fossanova. In 1323, Pope John XXII canonized him, while in 1567, Pope Pius V declared him a Doctor of the Church. Thomism, derived from his doctrines, retains an important role in Roman Catholic education and contemporary thought.

Suggested Readings

Jenkins, John I. *Knowledge and Faith in Thomas Aquinas* (1997).
Wippel, John F. *The Metaphysical Thought of Thomas Aquinas: From Finite Being to Uncreated Being* (2000).

10 Chapter

Eastern Empires

Suleiman the Magnificent

Known to Europeans as "the Magnificent," owing to his conquests and the opulence of his court, the Ottoman Sultan Suleiman I was called "the Lawgiver" by his own people because of his internal reforms. Suleiman greatly extended the area of Ottoman influence, pushing well up into the Balkan peninsula where his troops burned Budapest in 1526 and threatened Vienna, the heart of the Holy Roman Empire. What specific accomplishments led many contemporaries and later historians to consider Suleiman I to be the greatest Ottoman sultan?

* * *

When Sultan Selim I died in July 1520 as he prepared for a campaign against Hungary, he left for his successor a clear path to the sultan's throne. Years before, Selim, known to some as "the Grim," had taken the precaution of murdering not only his brothers, but also his sons and grandsons, save one. Suleiman, born in November 1494, assumed his father's throne secure from immediate challenge, thanks to Selim's foresight. The tradition of eliminating potential claimants to the Ottoman throne, as gruesome as it was, was accepted practice, intended to prevent struggles for power within the court. Years later, as sultan, Suleiman authorized the murder of his own son Mustafa; his wife Roxelana had convinced him that Mustafa, born to the sultan and another woman, had ambitions of overthrowing his father. From behind a screen, Suleiman watched as mute slaves strangled Mustafa with a bowstring, unaware that Roxelana had contrived the story of Mustafa's disloyalty so as to ensure the succession of one of her sons. Some time later, Suleiman later was compelled to order the murder of Roxelana's son Bayezid and five grandsons as a result of similar fears of conspiracy. The sultan's court at Constantinople was notorious for intrigue, and preemptive murder was often accepted as the only sure means of securing the throne or the succession to it.

This gruesome reality behind the outward magnificence of the Ottoman court was obscured by the numerous public accomplishments of Suleiman the Magnificent. Determined to win the loyalty of his subjects, Suleiman ended a number of unpopular measures soon after assuming power. Trade with Iran was reopened. Craftsmen and intellectuals who had been forcibly brought to Constantinople from other parts of the empire were given leave to depart. A new decree required that soldiers pay for all provisions taken during campaigns. New taxes were levied according to the ability to pay. The court system was enlarged even as administrative institutions were reorganized, with officials serving on the basis of merit and obligated to respect the rights of all subjects.

These early reforms did much to establish Suleiman's reputation as a just ruler but, as was the case throughout his reign, domestic issues were soon overshadowed by foreign affairs. As certain in his rectitude as were contemporary European rulers, Suleiman considered his empire to be a gift from God, and was determined to expand and defend it. Cognizant of the historical hostility of European states toward the Muslim East, and of the shrinking area under Islamic control, Suleiman undertook to destabilize Europe as much as possible. The Protestant Reformation presented the Ottoman sultan with the opportunity to weaken both the Roman church and western empires. Suleiman covertly funded Protestant powers in hopes of encouraging the internal divisions within European Christendom. Powerful opponents like the Holy Roman Empire could be weakened through such policies. It was also Suleiman's policy to support any Muslim country threatened by Christian Europe. Early in his reign, however, the challenges came not from Europe but from within the empire and on its periphery. In the 1520s, minor revolts flared not only in Syria but also in Egypt. In the latter, the Ottoman pasha Ibrahim, at Suleiman's urging, pursued a policy of relentlessly suppressing rebels while simultaneously demonstrating the sultan's benevolence and largesse to those who remained loyal. As in Anatolia, a broad range of reforms generally won the population over to Ottoman rule. Ibrahim's assignment in Egypt was illustrative of the institutionalization of the Ottoman social structure. The ruling class included those responsible for administration, finance, supervision of the military, and religious and cultural leadership duties. A vast subject class carried out most other state functions through autonomous religious communities called *millet* – which might be Muslim, Greek Orthodox, Jewish, or Armenian Christian, among other possibilities – and through artisan guilds, popular mystic orders and various confederations. The social structure of the Ottoman Empire, while having some elements in common with European countries, was in many ways unique, the product of centuries of tradition and accommodation.

The Ottoman tolerance of Christian communities within the Islamic empire continued despite the regular threats posed by Christian powers. In 1522, Suleiman was compelled to marshal his armies against the Knights of St. John of Jerusalem, a military religious order based on the island of Rhodes. The island supported a thriving pirate fleet that preyed on rich Ottoman cargo vessels. An Ottoman siege of the Knights' fort succeeded after Jewish and Muslim women enslaved by the Knights aided the besiegers in gaining entry to the fortress city. Defeated, the Knights were expelled, though other inhabitants were permitted to remain under the conditions of religious freedom allowed elsewhere in the empire. Such latitude was rarely granted to the vanquished by the Christian nations of Europe.

Suleiman's more immediate focus was, however, much farther north in Hungary. The Ottoman thrust into Europe began early in his reign, as Ottoman forces sought to eliminate Christian outposts along the southern banks of the Danube and Drava rivers in Serbia and Bosnia. In August 1520, Suleiman's armies took the fortress at Belgrade and thus secured most of Serbia. Ottoman fortunes seemed to improve further when antagonism between the French and the Habsburgs engendered new divisions among the Christian powers. Though distracted by revolts in Anatolia, Ottoman forces advanced into Hungary in the spring of 1526. The campaign was disastrous for the Hungarian King Louis II, who, along with many of his advisors, was killed during the battle of Mohacs, which left the Ottomans in control of Buda and Pest. Because of the problems in the east, Suleiman decided against a full occupation of Hungary at this point. A second Hungarian campaign in 1529 brought Ottoman armies to the very walls of Vienna, the Habsburg capital. A number of circumstances led Suleiman to call off the siege before the city's surrender could be compelled; Ottoman armies were operating at the furthest possible terminus of their supply lines. While Vienna was saved, Suleiman succeeded in imposing his authority over much of Hungary, thus establishing a buffer zone between the Ottoman Empire and the Habsburgs. A third campaign into Hungary in 1532 did little to further Suleiman's goals, though it created the circumstances in which a useful alliance with France could be affirmed in 1535. In 1541, the Austrian Archduke Ferdinand sought to challenge Ottoman authority, provoking yet another Ottoman invasion that drove the Austrians back. The Habsburg call for a crusade to oust the Muslim invaders led to a fifth campaign in 1543, which ended with Suleiman in control of most of Hungary.

The French alliance against the Habsburgs drew the Ottoman Empire into a series of raids in the western Mediterranean in the early 1540s, and Ottoman fleets assaulted the Italian coast before arriving in southern France. Though the Ottoman fleet was exuberantly welcomed, relations with France soured shortly afterwards as the French king lost his enthusiasm for continuing the struggle against the Habsburgs. A French-Habsburg truce in 1545 led Suleiman to conclude that a general peace might be beneficial and, as of 1547, the French, the Habsburgs and the Ottomans all turned to internal affairs. The Ottomans, however, held naval supremacy in the Mediterranean.

During the next five years, Suleiman pursued many of the reforms that earned him the honorific name *Kanuni*, or lawgiver. The organization and hierarchy of religious and cultural institutions were further defined. Precise regulations governing the role and activities of the *ulema*, the religious scholars, were devised, granting them control over all formal education. The *ulema* provided free education to Muslim boys. Suleiman also oversaw the codification and modernization of the legal code. In addition to regulations for markets, guilds, prices, wages and trade laws, the updated legal code imposed fines instead of physical punishment for many crimes. During this same period, Suleiman's patronage of artists, writers and architects further enhanced his reputation as an enlightened ruler.

As was often the case, imperial problems superseded domestic affairs. Suleiman was compelled to deploy forces to Iran with only problematic success and later sent armies into Transylvania in the early 1550s, where a lengthy struggle against Habsburg ambitions continued intermittently for a decade, with no decisive gains for any of the belligerents. At the same time, the struggle against the Habsburg Emperor Charles V was renewed in the Mediterranean, where Turkish fleets again raided the Italian coast. Growing religious conflict within the Holy Roman Empire led Charles to seek peace with the Ottomans in 1562. The Ottoman fleet remained busy elsewhere, however, extending the sultan's authority into the Red Sea during the 1550s.

By the 1560s, the strain of decades of warfare was becoming evident in the empire's stretched finances and weakening economy. Signs of growing political discontent, an inevitable outgrowth of both court intrigue and challenges to imperial authority, were increasingly worrisome. Suleiman the Magnificent died in September 1566 in the course of yet another Hungarian campaign. The seventy-two-year-old sultan left behind an empire that included not only Anatolia, but also much of the Balkans, North Africa and the Middle East. His fleet was still the dominant power in the Mediterranean. He had gone far toward his ambitions of making Constantinople the center of an expanded Islamic empire renowned for its culture as well as its military prowess. Unfortunately, his son and successor, Selim II failed to maintain Suleiman's legacy and the Ottoman Empire began a slow but perceptible decline over the next three and a half centuries.

Suggested Reading

Shaw, Stafford. *History of the Ottoman Empire and Modern Turkey* (1976).
Whearcroft, Andrew. *The Ottomans* (1996).

Ivan IV, "The Terrible"

Sometimes described as the first true Russian tsar, Ivan IV is remembered most for his capricious rule and personal viciousness. While subjecting Russia to a virtual reign of terror, Ivan IV simultaneously set about completing the evolution of Muscovite Russia into an empire. With the intention of establishing Orthodox Russia as a "Third Rome," Ivan the Dread extended Russia rule and committed his country to a succession of wars. How successful was Ivan in accomplishing his goals? What were the negative consequences of his rule?

* * *

Ivan IV was three years old at the time of the death of his father Vassily III in 1533. The consolidation of Muscovite Russia had been greatly advanced during previous decades. His grandfather, Ivan III (1462–1505) had pushed the boundaries of the Grand Duchy of Moscow to the north, incorporating the city-state of Novgorod, and to the south and east, pushing retreating Mongol forces back to the Volga River. Vassily had continued this policy of expansion, sometimes with more problematic success. But by the early sixteenth century, the core of a potentially powerful Russian empire had been secured. Ivan IV's great objective, which was sometimes subordinated to palace intrigues and his mercurial temper, was to make Russia the dominant eastern Christian empire.

The succession to the Russian throne was then, as it would be in centuries to come, contentious and the authority of the infant Ivan was soon challenged by princes determined to restore authority that had been lost to Moscow in previous decades. Nonetheless, Ivan's mother Helen, a member of the important Glinsky family, governed as regent, having won the allegiance of a group of boyars, powerful aristocrats who aided her effort to maintain the throne's authority. The earliest years of Ivan's life at court were rife with conspiracies, arrests and murders as palace intrigues swirled around the young tsar. Helen died in 1538, perhaps poisoned by a conspirator. In her absence, Ivan was often callously treated by the boyars and was witness to the political tumult and frequent cruelty that typified life at court. Contemporaries suggest that the sadistic behavior of later years was evident in Ivan even at this early point. As he matured, sexual license joined capricious brutality as chief behavioral traits. Ironically, as one historian notes, "his depravity in no way interfered with his deep piety." Prone to bouts of morbid religiosity, Ivan was determined to advance the status of the Russian Orthodox Church, though in a direction and by means that he would determine.

In 1547, Ivan was crowned Tsar of All the Russias, a title claimed by earlier rulers, but one that was never before officially conferred. Shortly afterwards, Ivan eliminated the boyars from his inner council, appointing a new "selected council" of non-aristocrats as part of an early bid to assert his independence. He was a man of considerable paradox. Despite his already severe nature at age seventeen, Ivan was one of the most literate of Russian rulers, both a voluminous reader and prolific writer. He was the first Russian tsar to advocate and expound on the doctrine of absolutism, maintaining that he ruled by divine right and that no temporal authority superseded his. He also held the Russian church to be subordinate to his will and in several instances dealt with insufficiently obedient church officials in the harshest fashion. During the 1570s, following a punitive expedition against Novgorod, the archbishop Leonid was murdered, either strangled or, as one account has it, sewn into a bearskin and tossed to savage dogs. Throughout his reign, Ivan was quick to punish troublesome clerics and confiscate church property. No respecter of the sanctity of the church, Ivan was not averse to having his victims murdered in church, sometimes during mass.

Among Ivan's accomplishments were a number of domestic reforms. At the central government level, he authorized the *zemskii sobor*, a consultative assembly representing Russia's social orders: the clergy, the boyars, the service class (estate owners), and merchants. The body was not meant to provide popular representation and could at most only advise the tsar, whose power remained absolute. Ivan also introduced new administrative agencies known as *prikasy*, intended to strengthen central administrative control. At the provincial level, efforts to make governors more accountable to local electorates were initiated; freemen were given the obligation of electing judicial and police authorities. The drawback was that the community as a whole was then held responsible for public safety and could face fines in the event of criminal activity. During the 1550s, financial administration was turned over to local administrative bodies known as *zemstvos*, which were comprised of elected officials. This was not so much an effort to expand local self-government as to make local administrative bodies, and the communities they represented, directly responsible for financial matters like taxes and dues. Again, communities were responsible for individual malfeasance. A decree of 1556 redefined the obligations of estate owners to the government, so as to ensure that each did his part in meeting the state's military needs, providing both men and personal service.

Ivan's desire to establish Russia as the dominant Christian empire led him to pursue a variety of religious reforms. A "Hundred Chapters" council confirmed the low quality of the Russian clergy, who were notorious for corruption, illiteracy, debauchery and disregard for the welfare of their parishioners. Unfortunately, though such problems were acknowledged, no effort to resolve them was made. The corrupting influence of ecclesiastical estates and immensely valuable church property was also never adequately resolved; church officials remained steadfast in their determination to retain their worldly holdings. Instead, the leader of the Church, the Metropolitan Macarius, sought to bolster the status of the Russian church through the mass canonization of saints; in the 1540s, more saints were added to the church calendar than in the previous five hundred years. Ultimately, any significant church reform was subordinated to discussion of relatively trivial matters, such as how the sign of the cross was to be made.

Ivan's reforms were not motivated by any concern for the lot of his people; he pursued reforms that would enhance the administrative efficiency and strength of his empire. Those who sought to appeal to his sense of justice ran considerable risks. A group of imminent men from Pskov, who petitioned Ivan to remedy their grievances against an arbitrary provincial governor, instead fell victim to his unpredictable wrath. They were doused with boiling wine, and then their beards and hair were burned before they were compelled to lie naked on the floor. Only the coincidental loud fall of a nearby church bell distracted Ivan, thereby sparing the unfortunate men from further tortures.

Territorial expansion was one of Ivan's major goals and in the course of his reign, Russia engaged in numerous conflicts with varying degrees of success. One major concern involved the Tatar states to the southeast, and in 1552 Ivan led a successful invasion of Kazan, which was annexed to Russia. Astrakhan was conquered in 1556, but the Russians struggled for years afterwards to subjugate the tribes of their now extended borderlands. Ultimately, however, the whole of the Volga basin was brought under Moscow's control. To the south, however, the Crimean Tatars posed a continuing if intermittent threat, and Ivan enlisted Cossacks as frontier forces to prevent their unpredictable incursions. Nonetheless, in 1571, a large Tatar force pushed all the way to Moscow, ultimately burning part of the city and hauling away 150,000 captives. Russian defenses were weakened due to a concurrent war in the west, where Russian forces had been struggling to seize Livonia since 1558. There, a war against the German knights who controlled portions of the Baltic coast grew more complex over time as a number of western powers were drawn into the quarrel. Russian designs were thwarted by the emergence of a strengthened Polish–Lithuanian union in the late 1560s. The death of the Polish king in 1572 led Ivan to assert his claim to that throne and the Livonian War erupted anew. The conflict ended in 1582 with a restoration of the *status quo antebellum*; Russia was compelled to withdraw from most of the territories held since the 1550s and lost her foothold on the Baltic. Russian imperial designs fared better in the far north and east, where the Stroganov family sought to expand a trading empire. Though Ivan's government was initially unsupportive of this private venture, news of the conquest of much of western Siberia brought about a change in attitude and the tsar lent his approval to the movement east. By the 1580s, Russia's advance to the Pacific was underway.

Throughout these decades, the constants were Ivan's unpredictability and growing brutality, which were manifest in both his private and public life. When he sought his first bride, Ivan ordered nobles to send their daughters to be interviewed by provincial governors, who would then forward the names of the selectees to Moscow, where Ivan would make his choice. Anastasia, his first wife, was poisoned by an unknown hand, as were at least two others. Two were compelled to enter convents while a third was drowned on Ivan's orders. The exact number of his wives remains unknown. Perhaps most infamously, in 1581, Ivan, in an uncontrollable rage, struck and murdered his son when the boy tried to protect his mother from the tsar's fury. Suspicious to the point of paranoia, Ivan ordered the torture and execution of growing numbers of family, clergy, nobles and hapless commoners who caught his eye. An obsessive fear of plots led him to undertake a bizarre journey in 1564, when he fled Moscow, pledging never to return. Taking his family and the court to Aleksandrovskaia Sloboda, Ivan announced his intention to abdicate, blaming scheming boyars and clergymen for his decision. Petitions imploring him to return to Moscow changed his mind, and he agreed to return, if the government would foot the bill for his flight, the guilty boyars were executed, and a special domain was created for him.

This special domain, or *oprichnina*, was to be a territory directly controlled by the tsar and any agencies he might devise. The remainder of the nation was the *zemshchina*, administered by traditional institutions. The intention was to free Ivan from the machinations of traitors and to end the political influence of the aristocracy. To accomplish these goals, Ivan's agents, the *oprichniki*, were given broad authority and functioned as agents of the security police. To strike fear into the hearts of arrogant aristocrats, the *oprichniki* carried two symbols of their purpose—a broom and, attached to their saddles, a dog's head. Under this new regime, boyars and landed aristocrats were deprived of their estates and deported to distant provinces. The tsar's residence at Aleksandrovskaia Sloboda became infamous as the center of this frightful regime. There, Ivan and his favorites tempered the tedium of lengthy church services with periodic orgies and torture sessions. In 1574, Ivan inexplicably named a Tatar prince as Russian tsar, though the man never exercised power and was eventually exiled. Historians are at a loss to explain this bizarre act.

Ivan IV died in 1584, after having taken monastic vows in his deathbed. His reign was marked by unprecedented cruelties, though he introduced some domestic reforms that could be said to have improved administrative efficiency. His often-irrational behavior did not prevent him from successfully extending the Russian empire, though he was not always victorious in war. Centuries later, the Soviet dictator Joseph Stalin indicated his admiration for the tsar who controlled and shaped an immense country through the use of terror. Soviet historians cited the *oprichnina* as historical precedent for Stalin's massive collectivization of land, and the destruction of the landed peasantry in the 1930s.

Suggested Reading

Florinsky, Michael T. Russia: *A History and an Interpretation* (1953).
Graham, Stephen. *Ivan the Terrible* (1933).

11

Chapter

Warriors in the Late Middle Ages

Henry V, King of England

The era of the Hundred Years' War produced a prodigious number of heroes and villains, the courageous and the craven, but few established a legacy as enduring as that of Henry V. English contemporaries celebrated his numerous virtues and he was soon immortalized in Shakespeare's play bearing his name as the title. Centuries later, he was hailed in Victorian England as the model of a Christian gentleman. Even among many modern historians, Henry V is lauded as a remarkable monarch; historian K.B. Mc-Farlane concluded that Henry was "the greatest man who ever ruled England." Henry's reputation stems from his strong personality and military genius, which served him well in restoring civil order in England and successfully asserting the Lancastrian claim to French land. What specific achievements established this king's legendary reputation?

* * *

Henry of Monmouth, as he was known at his birth, entered the world in the gatehouse of Monmouth Castle in South Wales in September 1387. He was the child of Henry Bolingbroke, whose ambitions later drastically altered the course of the young Henry's life, and the wealthy heiress Mary Bohun. Bolingbroke was the son of John of Gaunt, Duke of Lancaster. Henry was first cousin to the reigning King Richard II, a relationship that did not necessarily ensure his personal safety in an era of court intrigue. Henry's early years were not well chronicled because there were no unusual expectations for his future. He shared a bedroom with his brothers and was tutored by his uncle Henry Beaufort; as an adult he possessed a considerable library and was given to reading history, religious works and literature, including the works of his contemporary Chaucer. As a youth, he indulged in the pastimes common to the nobility, most notably hunting and falconry. Henry also demonstrated an affinity for music and learned to play the harp.

By 1398, Henry was drawn into events of his father's making when he was summoned to the court of Richard II. There he was held as a virtual hostage. The king had pronounced a sentence of banishment on Henry's father, in part as retribution for Bolingbroke's part in ruining the political prospects of Richard II's favorites a decade before, and perhaps more so to facilitate Richard's confiscation of Bolingbroke's considerable inheritance. The quarrel between the king and his father left Henry in a precarious position, which was emphasized later in the year when the king led an expedition to subdue Ireland and took the Henry with him as a hostage. The campaign proved disastrous, even more so when word came that Bolingbroke had returned to England to reclaim the duchy of Lancaster. Henry was left behind in Ireland when Richard returned to England. Bolingbroke's return was greeted with enthusiasm by many who were alienated by Richard's arbitrary and often incompetent rule and the king soon found himself literally outnumbered and surrounded at Conway Castle in northern Wales. Captured and incarcerated in the Tower in London, Richard was compelled to abdicate. Parliament compliantly declared the throne vacant and Bolingbroke assumed the crown as Henry IV in October 1399.

While Henry of Monmouth was now the presumptive heir, his father's arguably spurious claim to the throne shaped the lives of both. Though much of the public had supported Bolingbroke's claim to Lancaster, important elements of the landed aristocracy were uncomfortable with his seizure of the throne and many feared that they had only exchanged a weak and malleable monarch for a more determined and competent ruler. Thus much of Henry IV's reign was devoted to crushing previous allies and demonstrating his own fitness to rule through frequent military campaigns. The intermittent wars of these years had considerable impact on young Henry's character and perspective, shaping the later warrior-king who committed his country to yet another phase of the Hundred Years' War. As early as August 1400, Henry IV began a campaign aimed at compelling the King of Scots to pay homage, and Prince Henry, at age thirteen, was given command of a small group of foot soldiers and archers. The expedition was unsuccessful and shortly after its return to England, a rebellion broke out in Wales. As soon became evident, the Welsh uprising was part of a complex and lengthy enterprise undertaken by the earl of Northumberland, Sir Edmund Mortimer and Owen Glendower for the purpose of dividing much of the kingdom between them. The plotting touched off a half dozen years of conflict, during which Prince Henry gained considerable experience, both as a soldier and as military governor of Wales. The long struggle finally ended in

1409, with Northumberland executed, Glendower driven back into the Welsh marshes and Mortimer starved to death in the course of a siege at Harlech Castle.

Henry's youth was not entirely given over to serious endeavors. During these same years he established a reputation as a man who enjoyed the camaraderie of drinking companions and the company of women. Tales concerning his brawling, wenching ways were probably exaggerated, but nonetheless inspired Shakespeare's Falstaff, who claimed the friendship of "Prince Hal," described in Shakespeare's play as a "good shallow young fellow." Henry was acquainted with Sir John Fastolf, but he was a dour and rigid professional soldier, an unlikely model for Shakespeare's lighthearted princely companion.

Henry IV's efforts to firmly establish the Lancastrian claim to the throne were ultimately successful, but were achieved only at the cost of destabilizing English society, which was increasingly prone to lawlessness. Likewise, the incessant campaigns broke the king's health and in his later years he became increasingly neurotic, suffering from a form of eczema that many believed to be leprosy, a divine punishment. During Henry IV's last days, the enfeebled monarch was suspicious even of his own son, whose desire to rule in his own right was becoming more evident. His death in March 1413 brought his son to the throne as Henry V.

Contemporaries described the twenty-five-year-old king as exceptionally physically fit, as well as being self-confident, charismatic, energetic and thoroughly convinced that God endorsed his cause. Indeed, there is compelling evidence that Henry underwent a religious conversion about the time he became king. He gave up the habits of his tumultuous youth and adopted a more severe demeanor that was in keeping with his newfound piety. As monarch he was not tolerant of religious dissent, much less heresy, and was inclined to deal harshly with the troublesome Lollards. An anticlerical sect that rejected many aspects of Catholicism, the Lollards, led by John Oldcastle, rebelled in 1413. Oldcastle was driven into hiding and dozens of his fellow conspirators, once captured, suffered horrible deaths. Episodes such as this led less charitable sources to characterize Henry V as domineering, sanctimonious and bigoted. Whatever his other attributes, Henry clearly came to the throne with significant military skills. In the course of the lengthy Welsh campaigns, Henry had grown familiar with both siege craft and gunnery. He had also learned how best to hold conquered territory and how to utilize limited manpower resources most effectively. These skills would serve him well in his effort to reassert English claims in southwestern France.

The accession of Henry V marked the beginning of the third and last phase of the Hundred Years' War, which, since 1337, had drawn much of Europe's nobility into the lengthy struggle between the two monarchies. The war was a paradoxical conflict characterized by often-ritualized chivalric behavior as well as by brutal savagery. Henry V, who embodied many of these seemingly antagonistic qualities, was inevitably drawn to the prospect of the glory that renewed warfare with the French promised. France in 1414 was torn by civil unrest and weakened by an insane king, Charles VI. War against France also offered an opportunity to ameliorate some of England's social ills. Bored, potentially rebellious nobles and lawless criminals could both be put to more constructive tasks by serving in a new English army of conquest.

Accordingly, Henry determined to reassert the Plantagenet claim to the French throne and to seize it by force if necessary. He began preparing for the inevitable conflict in 1413, and after lengthy and convoluted diplomatic machinations, Henry essentially demanded that the French king surrender the Angevin empire to him. When the French rudely refused to comply, Henry declared war in August 1415, blaming Charles VI for the breakdown in negotiations. Henry assembled an army of 10,000, together with all of the weapons and machines of war at Southampton. This force was loaded aboard a fleet said by some to number 1500 vessels, which sailed for France on August 11. The English "armada" disembarked its troops at the channel port city of Harfleur, which gave up in September after a pounding by English artillery. Though Henry's army was relatively small in numbers and wearied by the campaign, the king insisted that his troops march overland through Normandy toward Calais. There, on October 25, Henry's men found themselves facing a French army perhaps five times their number. Though the immediate situation did not appear to favor the invaders, the battle of Agincourt was destined to be known as one of England's greatest feats of arms. The battleground, rain-soaked and cramped, proved unfavorable to the French, who were unable to capitalize on their numerical superiority. English archers wreaked devastating havoc on the French troops and at battle's end, Henry could claim a clear-cut military victory. Agincourt decimated the French nobility and the dead included three dukes, eight counts and 1500 knights, together with some 4,000–5,000 soldiers. Though the English lost the duke of York and the earl of Suffolk, less than 3,000 English dead were left on the field.

The French defeat at Agincourt, together with the inability of antagonistic noble factions to unite in defense of the kingdom, ensured that Henry would not only occupy Normandy but would also successfully press his claim to the throne. Philip, the son of John of Burgundy, allied with the English following his father's murder by the Orleanist faction. In 1420, Philip and Henry imposed the Treaty of Troy on a now-battered France. The treaty permitted Charles VI to retain his crown, but

Henry was given Catherine, the king's daughter, as his bride and was proclaimed the rightful heir to the French throne. Henry in return promised to defend all those parts of France that acknowledged the treaty, and to continue the struggle against those areas that remained loyal to the unfortunate and now disinherited royal heir, the *dauphin*. Parliament ratified the treaty in May 1420, thus establishing a dual kingdom. The future of the new realm was contingent on England's ability to defend it and French willingness to accept it. Henry did not live to inherit the French crown. He died in August 1422, two months before Charles VI. That left the nine-month old infant Henry VI as heir, and created the circumstances or a gradual revival of French resistance, which produced a heroine as dear to the French as Henry V was to the English. Joan of Arc would play a central role in the final phase of the Hundred Years' War, which would finally see the English ejected from France.

Suggested Readings

Harriss, G.L., editor. *Henry V* (1985).
Seward, Desmond. *Henry V: The Scourge of God* (1987).

Joan of Arc, Maid of Orléans

The Hundred Years' War produced one of France's greatest national heroines, Joan of Arc. Her reputation endures not only because of her role in the third and last phase of the war, but because of her martyrdom to her cause, expelling the English from France. In the decades after her death, the legend of her divinely sanctioned mission was firmly established in France and strengthened over several centuries. In 1920, Pope Benedict XV canonized her as St. Joan. What was Joan's role in the Anglo-French conflict? What brought about her execution?

* * *

Joan d'Arc (sometimes Darc) was born to peasant parents in the village of Domrémy in 1412. Her father Jacques supported his daughter and a wife Isabelle by farming and though the family had few material possessions, they were not impoverished. There is surprisingly significant information about Joan's childhood, largely because of the revision of her 1431 trial in the 1450s. At that point, numerous acquaintances offered extensive testimony as to her early years. What emerged is a portrait of a not unusual child who engaged in the female activities that one would normally associate with French village life, sewing, cooking, and spinning. Like most of her peers, Joan did not learn to read or write. These same years marked the beginning of the final phase of the Hundred Years' War. The deaths of England's Henry V and France's Charles VI left the arrangements made in the wake of the French defeat at Agincourt in doubt, and the country was soon divided, with the dauphin, later Charles VII, ruling central France with the support of the Armagnacs and the Duke of Burgundy holding a vast territory in the northeast. These circumstances permitted the Duke to broker peace or war, by alternately seeking English or French support for his ambitions. Joan's village was within the Duke's territory, but remained loyal to the dauphin's party. At points the war brushed the small village, as in 1419 when Joan's father, together with another family, jointly rented a fortress on an island in the Meuse River which could serve as sanctuary for the villagers and their livestock should a threat materialize.

In the summer of 1424 (some sources say 1425), at a point when the war was going badly for the dauphin, Joan, then thirteen, experienced the first of a series of supernatural manifestations that recurred throughout her life. She told of hearing voices and seeing a blaze of light, phenomena that she later identified as emanating from angels. Though the "celestial voices" continued for several years, they did not reveal a specific mission until 1428, at which point Joan insisted that she was being urged to offer her help to the dauphin, now Charles VII. She traveled to the nearby village of Vaucouleurs, where she presented her message to Robert Baudricourt, the local royal commander. Baudricourt, a hard-bitten soldier, was skeptical of Joan's story and sent her back home, telling the cousin who had accompanied her, "Take her home to her father and give her a good whipping."

Joan was undeterred however, as her voices became more insistent and the French military situation deteriorated. Though she implored the voices that she was no soldier and could not ride or fight, they were insistent. "It is God who commands it," she later recounted the voices saying. In January 1429, she again headed for Vaucouleurs. Baudricourt's earlier skepticism had not lessened, but as Joan remained in the town, she told of a vision of a terrible French defeat outside Orléans. When the disaster at the battle of Herrings was known several days later, Joan's credibility was greatly strengthened. Joan was permitted to proceed to Chinon to see the king; it was at this point that she adopted male attire, perhaps because it was better suited to horseback travel and to protect her modesty in all-male military encampments. She met with Charles VII in early March and the monarch tested her by disguising himself among his attendants. Joan unerringly identified him, sparking a heated controversy with the king's court as to whether the teenaged girl was "God's messenger" or a lunatic. Joan supposedly gained the king's trust by showing him "a secret sign," according to some sources, information that would assure the king's private doubts as to the legitimacy of his birth.

Joan's insistence that she was given a divine mission to save France from the English led to her examination by a panel of bishops and academicians, who were evidently convinced of the legitimacy of her claim. She returned to Chinon, where she fully assumed the role of warrior-maid, outfitting herself in armor as she made preparations for a campaign against the English. She refused the sword offered her by the king and asked instead to be allowed to search for an ancient sword said to be buried behind a chapel altar in Saint-Catherine de-Fierbois. Legend holds that Joan's voices guided her to the fabled sword. Shortly afterwards, she was presented with her standard, a white banner depicting God's blessing of the French cause. On the eve of the campaign, Joan revealed another vision affirming French victory, the coronation of Charles VII and numerous other details. In late April, Joan and her army arrived at Orléans, where they soon ended an English siege. Though the king's advisor's were reluctant, Joan gained approval for another campaign in the Loire valley, where the English were again defeated at Patay. French forces, at Joan's urging, pushed on to Reims, where Charles VII was crowned on July 17, 1429, with Joan in attendance.

To this point, Joan seemed triumphant, but her pronounced desire to continue the campaign against the English met with considerable opposition from the king's advisers. To Joan, Charles and his court must have seemed irresolute, failing to follow up victories, jumping to every diplomatic lure tossed by the Duke of Burgundy and generally hesitating when bold decisions were required. Thus, it was in 1430 that Joan undertook another campaign with little support from the king, this time assaulting Paris in early September. Though Joan performed heroically, suffering a crossbow bolt shot into her thigh, the attack failed and the effort was abandoned. The failure encouraged Joan's opponents at court and weakened the credibility of her claims to divine sanction. Charles VII soon after signed a truce with the treacherous Duke of Burgundy and Joan was compelled to forsake arms for the moment.

The reluctance of Charles VII to aggressively pursue the war against the English lessened the momentum of Joan's crusade. Compelled to spend much of the winter at court among superficial and often treacherous courtiers, Joan found little encouragement, other than the king's decision to ennoble her family. Only in April, when the truce expired, was Joan able to renew the campaign against France's enemies. That same month, her voices revealed that she would soon be taken prisoner. Indeed, on May 24, 1430, she was captured near Compiégne. Burgundian soldiers pulled her from her horse during the battle and she was made the prisoner of John of Luxembourg, who soon sold her to the English. The English were handed to golden opportunity to be rid of the woman who had inspired much of the renewed French resistance. If she could be pronounced a heretic and sorceress, the cloak of divine sanction, which had theretofore shielded her, would be cast aside. Joan of Arc's political and military activities, together with her male attire, placed her well outside the usual bounds of accepted gender roles and there were many who felt that those transgressions alone justified punishment. Her death would of course serve both the English and Burgundian causes. She was taken to Rouen for trial, where the appointed instrument of her destruction was Pierre Cauchon, Bishop of Beauvois, an accomplice of the Burgundian party.

The proceedings against Joan, who was under English guard at Rouen Castle prison, began in January 1431 and lasted into May. The conditions of her incarceration were harsh and she was often kept in an iron cage with her neck, hands and feet chained. During interrogations, she was questioned as to the nature of her visions, with the hope of revealing heretical thoughts. The theologians and academicians who assessed her ultimately settled on twelve "propositions" of misdeeds and then declared her voices to be "false and diabolical." In essence, Joan's heresy was in believing that she was directly responsible to God rather than to the Roman Catholic Church. Her adoption of male attire was also denounced. Condemned to die, she finally broke and confessed her errors, whereupon her sentence was reduced to life imprisonment. The English and Burgundians protested this leniency, but were reassured by Cauchon that Joan's life would yet be forfeited. Indeed, in prison Joan soon returned to wearing male apparel, a seemingly trivial lapse that nonetheless allowed for her retrial as a lapsed heretic. Condemned to death on May 29, Joan met her end the following day. The punishment for heresy was burning at the stake, and contemporaries record that Joan suffered the terrible death courageously. Her ashes were dumped into the River Seine.

One of Joan's final predictions was the defeat of the English, and following a treaty between Charles VII and the Duke of Burgundy in 1435, a unified French nation succeeded in expelling the English by 1453. Even before the end of the Hundred Years' War, Joan's case was being reassessed and in 1455 a 'trial of rehabilitation" was held at Paris' Notre Dame. The following year, the initial verdict condemning Joan was rescinded. In the centuries that followed, Joan of Arc's status as a French national heroine grew, and the formal process of canonization began in 1903. Though historians have long debated the nature and origins of her visions, there is little question of her enduring symbolic importance, both for the French and for Catholics.

Suggested Readings

Pernoud, Régine, editor. *Joan of Arc: By Herself and Her Witnesses* (1966).
Warner, Marina. *Joan of Arc: The Image of Female Heroism* (1981).

12 Chapter

Renaissance Thought

Niccolo Machiavelli

Deemed the father of modern political science, Niccolo Machiavelli, produced the masterpiece, The Prince, his volume on statecraft. Machiavelli contended that political determinations should not be controlled by spiritual and moral considerations. Highly controversial during his own lifetime, his views subjected to him to imprisonment, torture, and exile; following his death, The Prince was condemned by the Pope. How did Machiavelli's ideas help to shape the modern world? Why have his ideas proven so controversial?

* * *

Niccolo di Bernardo dei Machiavelli was born in Florence on May 3, 1469, the son of a well-known lawyer, Bernardo di Niccolo Buoninsegna, and Barolommea di Stefano Nelli. Both Bernardo and Barolommea belonged to old noble families based in Florence, but Bernardo's own family had fallen on hard economic times. Later, Machiavelli wrote that he "was born in poverty and at an early age learned how to endure hardship rather than flourish." Nevertheless, he must have been exposed to some of the great works that were published during the Renaissance, including the writings of Greek and Roman philosophers, along with Italian histories, from the small library that Bernardo held. In his *History of Florence*, Machiavelli painted a picture of how young men, perhaps like himself, spent their days under Medicean rule.

> They were freer than their forefathers in dress and living, and spent more in other kinds of excesses, consuming their time and money in idleness, gaming, and women; their chief aim was to appear well dressed and to speak with wit

83

and acuteness, whilst he who could wound others the most cleverly was thought the wisest.

At the time of Machiavelli's birth, Italy was experiencing political tumult. Four strong, but small city-states dominated Italian political life, although each in turn was beset by threats from other European governments. Beginning in 1434, the powerful and wealthy Medici family governed Florence, but near the end of the century a reform campaign briefly threatened their hold on power. In 1494, as the power of Piero de'Medici diminished, Machiavelli became involved with public service. In addition, Machiavelli may well have participated in the ouster of the Savonarolist regime four years later, which resulted in the execution of Girolamo Savonarola, the Dominican monk who had established a Florentine republic. When a new republic was constructed under chief magistrate Piero Soderni, Machiavelli received an appointment to head the newly formed government's Second Chancery, and to act as secretary of an agency that dealt with issues involving war and peace.

Serving in those capacities, he conducted a series of diplomatic missions in European courts. In 1499, he went to see Catherine Sforza, while the next year he traveled to France to obtain support from Louis XII in a campaign against Pisa. In 1502, Machiavelli visited Cesare Borgia, Pope Alexander VI's son, who served as the Duke Valentino. Following the death of Pius III in 1503, Machiavelli traveled to Rome to witness the papal election. After heading for France the next year, he returned to Rome in 1506 to speak with Pope Julius II. In 1507 and 1508, Machiavelli was an envoy at the court of Holy Roman Emperor Maximilian. One important achievement that Machiavelli brought about was the establishment of a standing army, which proceeded to retake control of Pisa in 1509.

In 1512, however, the Medici regained power, thanks to Spanish involvement, leading to Machiavelli's dismissal on November 7 and subsequent charges that he had conspired against the Medici family. Imprisoned, Machiavelli was tortured, before Leo X obtained his release. Although pardoned, Machiavelli was exiled to his small country estate at San Cascinao, close to Florence, where he spent much of his time writing, soon producing *The Prince, Discourse on the First Decade of Titus Livius, Florentine Histories,* and a pair of plays.

In correspondence written in late 1513, Machiavelli explained how he spent his evenings in his study, after he changed out of his "peasant-clothes" and attired himself in "noble court dress."

Thus becomingly re-clothed I pass into the ancient courts of the men of old, where, being lovingly received by them, I am fed with that food which is mine alone; where I do not hesitate to speak with them, and to ask for the reason of their actions, and they in their benignity answer me; and for four hours I feel no weariness. I forget every trouble, poverty does not dismay, death does not terrify me; I am possessed entirely by those great men. And because Dante says: 'Knowledge doth come of learning well retained, Unfruitful else ... .'

That year, Machiavelli wrote *The Prince*, which he did not publish during his lifetime. As revealed in a letter found three centuries later, Machiavelli drafted this treatise to curry favor with the ruling Medici. The book attempted to explain how power was won and then maintained, while indicating that any means, no matter how ignoble, were justified. In contrast to most political writers of his age, Machiavelli avoided an idealistic religious approach, seeking rather to examine government affairs in a realistic fashion. He challenged the classical views of Aristotle, which insisted that politics were the extension of ethics; some scholars suggest that Machiavelli applied a scientific method to the political arena. Regardless, many have accused Machiavelli of championing manipulative practices. As he produced *The Prince*, Italy remained beholden to foreign states, which, in his estimation, necessitated the forming of potent Italian city-states.

Machiavelli indicated that monarchies and republics were the two chief forms of governments of his age, but he concentrated on the former. A prince, Machiavelli believed, must be instructed by *virtu*, which he considered a mixture of talent and shrewdness, in his efforts to preserve his state. Such a leader should acquire a reputation for stinginess, rather than generosity; should be viewed as harsh, not merciful; was best served by being considered severe, not merciful; but should avoid being hated to prevent his ouster. When necessary, the prince should employ deceit, although that should not be obvious to his public, which needed to consider him honest, upright, and religious. He should also be ready to employ cruelty and force, if necessary. A single misstep, he warned, could cost a ruler dearly, by dissipating his hard-won authority. As depicted in *The Prince,* social and political affairs remained highly problematic, leading Machiavelli to contend that calculated, manipulated thought and action were demanded.

In 1518, Machiavelli was hired to attend to the affairs in Genoa of a group of merchants from Florentine. The next year saw something of a relaxation in the Medici's iron-fisted control in Florentine. Machiavelli was among a group of individuals consulted about a constitution that would allow for the restoration of the Great Council, adapted from the representative body in Venice. That same year,

Leo X commissioned Machiavelli to produce a history of Florence. From 1521-1525, Machiavelli once again served in the diplomatic corps and as a historiographer. After the Emperor Charles VII defeated the French at Pavia in 1525, Machiavelli attempted to prevent the invading army from coursing through Florence on its way to sack Rome. In the spring of 1527, the Medici again lost power and a new republic was proclaimed, but an ailing Machiavelli was not allowed to participate in that reform campaign nor given a new position. Distrusted by the latest republican government, the fifty-eight year-old writer, political theorist, and former government official died on June 22. Three years later, a campaign joined by Emperor Charles VII and Pope Clement VII terminated the Third Republic of Florence. *The Prince* was published in 1532 but soon was condemned by the papacy. In 1564, Machiavelli's writings were included in the Church Index of books that were officially banned.

Suggested Readings

De Grazia, Sebastian. *Machiavelli in Hell* (1994).
Viroli, Maurizio. *Machiavelli* (1998).

Desiderius Erasmus

The Dutch humanist and theologian, Desiderius Erasmus became Europe's most renowned scholar and the first to obtain prominence thanks to the printing press. Copies of his voluminous works appeared across the European continent, helping to spread his message of the need to both challenge Church practices and return to the "philosophy of Christ." Befriended by leading intellectuals throughout Europe, his message helped to set the stage for the Protestant Reformation. How did the Renaissance influence Erasmus? Why did he become such an important figure in European intellectual history?

* * *

Desiderius Erasmus was born in Rotterdam, Holland, on October 28, in the middle of the 1460s, probably 1466. He was the illegitimate child of Roger Gerard, from Gouda, who later became a priest, and Margaretha Rogers, the daughter of a physician. Called Gerrit Gerritszoon, he eventually changed his name to the one he became known by Erasmus. Along with an older brother, Erasmus was brought up by Margaretha. At the age of nine, he was sent to Deventer to attend the school of the Brothers of the Common Life, soon most renowned for its stewardship by the well-regarded humanist Hegius. There, Erasmus's own fascination with humanism was piqued and his intellectual brilliance demonstrated. Margaretha died of the plague when Erasmus was only thirteen, while his father passed away shortly thereafter. For "two lost years," as he referred to them, Erasmus was enrolled in the monastery school of Hertogenbosch. A period of aimless wandering followed, which was terminated when his guardians, in 1486, demanded that he enter the monastery of Emmaus, close to Gouda. Lacking any sense of a religious calling at this point, Erasmus would consider this the most unfortunate period of his life. Despite such unhappy memories, Erasmus immersed himself in the ancient classics, whose elegance he admired. At the same time, he was trained in the work of St. Jerome, who had compiled the Vulgate, the Latin version of the Bible, and the humanist Lorenzo Valla.

Five years after he entered monastic life, Erasmus was able to escape from that existence. The Bishop of Cambrai intended to travel to Italy and desired a secretary and traveling companion. Erasmus's linguistic abilities endeared him to the bishop, who also ensured that he was ordained as a priest when he took his monastic vows in 1492. While the trip never panned out, Erasmus remained close to the bishop, who, in either 1495 or 1496, helped him attend the University of Paris as a theology student. Once again, Erasmus was unhappy with his academic environment, resulting in his rapid departure. Instead, Erasmus again displayed wanderlust, passing through France and the Netherlands. Serving as tutor for three Englishmen afforded him the funds and a letter of introduction to travel to England. There, in the final years of the fifteenth century, Erasmus encountered a series of individuals with whom he would carve out lifetime friendships with, including Thomas More, John Colet, and William Grocynthe. While at Oxford, Erasmus learned from Colet how he might retain his belief in humanism, discard the scholastic method, and explore religious texts.

Influenced by his new acquaintances, Erasmus returned to Paris and Louvain, where he studied Greek and began to publish his first writings. In 1500, the *Adagia*, which contained Greek and Latin proverbs, appeared. Two years later, so too did the *Manual (or Dagger) of the Christian Gentleman*, which condemned formalism and its fixation on traditions, rather than the true lessons of Christ. The answer, Erasmus indicated, was for each individual to determine what was most essential. In 1505, Erasmus saw to the release of Lorenzo Valla's *Annotiones* to the New Testament, which he had found at a monastery in Brussels. Particularly telling was Erasmus's introduction, a call for a literal rereading of Scriptures. Then, in 1506, he was able to go to Italy, something he had long desired. Accorded honors along the way, Erasmus was granted the Doctor of Divinity degree, while in other leading academic stations of northern Italy--Bologna, Padua, and Venice--he was warmly welcomed by renowned humanists. In Rome, the hearty reception continued, with the cardinals demonstrating great pleasure on greeting him. Declining ecclesiastical appointments, Erasmus evidently hoped to receive one in England, where Henry VIII had taken over.

Having met up with his friend Thomas More in 1509, Erasmus wrote *The Praise of Folly*, his biting critique of medieval society, especially Church abuses and excesses. Erasmus also castigated the sale of indulgences by the Church. He deemed merchants "the biggest fool(s) of all. They carry on the most sordid business and by the most corrupt methods." Nevertheless, "flattering friars" catered to them, desiring "some of the loot." Philosophers "know nothing, yet profess to know everything." As for theologians, Erasmus suggested it might be best to consider them "in silence." That short-tempered and supercilious crew is unpleasant to deal with," he observed, "is unpleasant to deal with." Admittedly, Erasmus continued, "They will proclaim me a heretic. With this thunderbolt they terrify the people they don't like. Their opinion of themselves is so great that they behave as if they were already in heaven; they look pityingly on other men as so many worms." Then, there were the self-proclaimed religious sorts and the monks. In reality, Erasmus noted, "Both are complete misnomers, since most of them stay as far away from religion as possible, and no people are seen more often in public." Afflicted with illiteracy, they were dirty, ignorant, boorish, and insolent. Monks of various orders viewed money with "horror ... as if it were poison, but not from wine or women. ... Most of them consider one heaven an inadequate reward for their devotion to ceremony and traditional details. They forget that Christ will condemn all of this and will call for a reckoning of that which He has prescribed, namely, charity." Even popes, Erasmus pointedly indicated, should attempt to imitate Christ, opting for lives of poverty and labor.

Remaining in England for the next five years, Erasmus refused a permanent appointment, electing instead to serve as a professor of Greek at Cambridge for a short while. Becoming disillusioned with Henry VIII's martial endeavors, he returned to the continent, ending up in Brabant to perform as a royal councilor for Archduke Charles, who later became Emperor Charles V. In 1516, Erasmus produced the *Institute Principis Christiania*, his words of advice to Charles. The Prince, Erasmus insisted, must be guided by honor and integrity, in his efforts to stand as the servant of the people. Erasmus soon returned to his travels, having received a papal dispensation. He spent a considerable amount of time in both England and Basle, where he encountered those who subscribed to the "new learning" and viewed him as a mentor.

Also published in 1516 was Erasmus's annotation of the New Testament, which included his critical commentary and appeared in Latin, while three years later, his work on St. Jerome was published. Challenging the capriciousness and heavy-handed approach of churchmen who subscribed to Scholasticism, Erasmus's treatments strove to present a more rational perception of Christian tenets. In a politically deft move, Erasmus dedicated his edition of the New Testament to Pope Leo X, but his own version of the New Testament could be viewed as another challenge to the authority of the Church. Erasmus was pleased that these volumes, like his other writings, were widely translated throughout Europe. Still, his message was largely intended for and received by scholarly elites, not common folk.

Clearly, the appeal of Erasmus's books, which suggested the need for the Church to undergo reform, helped to set the stage for more sweeping transformations. He viewed with disdain various church tenets, arguing instead for a simple interpretation of the Scriptures, and their interpretation by individuals. He praised the "philosophy of Christ," depicting it as a wholly ethical ideal that could be exemplified by human wisdom. But after Martin Luther posted his 95 Theses condemning indulgences on a church door in Wittenberg, Germany, in 1517, Erasmus was caught between the religious whirlwinds of change. Conservative forces assailed him as the source of the religious ferment that culminated in the schisms that divided the Church and resulted in the Protestant Reformation. He was also attacked by Lutherans, who viewed him as cowardly and for failing to pursue his analyses to their logical conclusions. Luther himself became more displeased with Erasmus, warning that "the human is of more value to him than the Divine." Still, Erasmus never favored the Church's attack on Luther or his excommunication. In 1521, Erasmus, who had hoped for the peaceful reform of the Church, felt compelled to depart from Louvain, having been rebuked by those who subscribed to standard Catholic tenets.

Erasmus settled in Basle, where he was welcomed by a good number of humanists. Nevertheless, he had to ward off criticisms from both conservative forces and Lutherans. The Lutherans, for their part, were enraged when Erasmus wrote *De Libero Arbitrio* (1523), criticizing Luther, whom he accused of denying free will. Luther responded with *De Servo Arbitrio* (1524), which challenged the humanism Erasmus held so dear. In the final years of his life, Erasmus, to his dismay, continued to be caught between contending religious forces. When Basle experienced the destruction of religious images, he departed to Freiburg, which remained Roman Catholic. He remained in good graces with the papacy, with Paul III even desiring to name him a cardinal, yet another honor Erasmus refused to accept. While back in Basle preparing to travel to Brabant in the Netherlands, Erasmus, who had just been informed that Sir Thomas More and Bishop Fischer had been executed, was afflicted with dysentery and died on July 12, 1536. In 1559, Erasmus's books were placed on the Inquisition's Papal Index of prohibited works.

Suggested Readings

Augustijn, Cornelis. *Erasmus: His Life, Works, and Influence* (1991).
Halkin, Leon-E. *Erasmus: A Critical Biography* (1993).
Huizinga, John. *Erasmus and the Age of Reformation,* (2001).

13
Chapter

Discovery and Knowledge

Christopher Columbus

Today, Christopher Columbus is sometimes reviled for having viewed indigenous peoples in the Caribbean through an ethnocentric lens, which resulted in brutal treatment being inflicted on them. At the same time, he remains the seafarer-navigator who helped to open up the Western hemisphere for European exploration and discovery. While Columbus never found the westward passage to the Orient he sought, his four voyages to the "New World" unveiled two continents whose bounty altered global politics and economics. How remarkable was Columbus feat when it occurred? Why was he considered a failure upon his death?

* * *

Christopher Columbus was born between August 25 and October 31, 1451, in Genoa, then serving as the capital of an independent Italian republic. His father, Domenico Columbus, was a wool weaver who was actively involved in his guild. His mother, Suzanna Fontanarossa, was herself the daughter of a wool weaver. Domenico and Suzanna had five children, of whom Christopher was the eldest. Columbus was particularly close to his brother Bartolomeo, with the two studying cartography together and yearning to complete a journey to the west. Columbus worked in the family trade of wool processing and marketing, and perhaps also toiled in a bookshop in Genoa for a time. He apparently had little formal schooling but later mastered Spanish and Latin on his own. In 1470, the Columbus family relocated to Savona, situated west of Genoa.

While it had been anticipated that the boys would pursue the same trade as their father, the sea beckoned. Some accounts indicate that Columbus worked as an errand boy, a sailor, and possibly as a privateer who conducted a mission to Tunis in 1472, or so his son Fernando later claimed. But historians dispute whether Columbus would have been placed in command of such an enterprise. It does appear that he sailed on a ship headed for Chios in the Aegean Sea in 1474. His return to Savona would be the last occasion that Columbus lived in the town where his family had come to reside. For a year, Columbus remained in Chios, which was undoubtedly still experiencing ripple effects from the turmoil in the region that had recently taken place. That was topped off, of course, by the Turkish conquest of Constantinople in 1451.

On August 13, 1476, Columbus was aboard the *Bechalla*, which was part of a school of five ships engaged in a commercial expedition to England. After passing through the Straits of Gilbraltrar, the convoy suffered an attack by French privateers, off the coast of Lagos, Portugal. Although wounded as his ship went down six miles from shore, Columbus, wielding an oar, managed to swim to land. Having recuperated, he went to a corner of Lisbon where a good number of merchants and ship-builders from Genoa could be found. Thanks to expeditions Prince Henry the Navigator had sponsored along the African coast, Lisbon had become a key center for entrepreneurs and adventurers alike. Bartolomeo joined Columbus in Lisbon, where the two became draftsmen dealing with cartography and also served as book collectors.

By 1477, however, Columbus was back at sea, sailing on a Portuguese ship bound for both Ireland and Iceland. Columbus possibly heard tales of Viking expeditions to the west of Iceland. Returning to Portugal, he met and wedded Felipa Perestrello e Moniz, a member of an esteemed, although financially bereft family of Portugal nobles. Felipa's deceased father, Bartolomeo—whose own family had arrived from Italy a century before—had been named hereditary governor of Porto Santo in the Madeiras Islands. Following the birth of their son Diego in 1480 or 1481, Felipa and Christopher went to dwell in Madeira, but she perished shortly thereafter.

Columbus continued to participate in a series of seagoing adventures, sailing to El Mina, a Portuguese fortress on the coast of Guinea and where riches, particularly gold, seemed to abound. The Portuguese sought a passage to the Orient, hoping to sail around the tip of Africa, believing they would encounter riches, including gold, gems, and spices. The alternative route involved a lengthy, arduous trek overland, but Columbus devised another plan. He envisioned sailing west, which purportedly would enable him to reach the Indies more quickly. In 1484, Columbus, relying on family access to the throne and boasting maps and documents obtained from his mother-in-law, implored King John II of Portugal to support his "Enterprise of the Indies." He requested three sailing vessels, a portion of any booty to be found, and governorship of lands he discovered. Columbus also wanted to be titled Admiral and to become a member of the Portuguese nobility.

The king, however, declined to accept Columbus's conditions, leading him to seek another patron: Spain. At the time, the Canary Islands represented Spain's only noteworthy imperial possession outside Europe. Columbus's initial efforts to elicit support from the Spanish crown also failed. Unable to garner financial sponsorship in both France and England, Columbus returned to Spain, which was battling the Moors. Having moved to Seville in 1485, he became involved with a peasant woman, Beatriz Enriquez de Arana, and in 1488, the two had a child, Fernando. For a period, Columbus was near economic destitution. However, after subduing Granada, the Moors' final Spanish stronghold, King Ferdinand and Queen Isabella proved willing to finance Columbus's voyage. The role played by Isabella, who had placed Columbus on the royal payroll, was considerable, as she foresaw multifold opportunities in his quest. Such an adventure, she believed, might allow for the gospel of Christianity to spread and would enable Spain to compete with Portugal for imperial supremacy. Thus, she willingly deferred to Columbus's requests, including the granting of honors and titles.

Columbus was relying on perceptions of the world that were both ancient and of recent vintage. Columbus subscribed to an idea then current, shaped by Paolo del Pozzo Toscanelli of Florence, that a maritime voyage of approximately 3000 miles could carry one to the East; this contested Ptolemy's theory that the distance was three times greater. Bartolome de las Casas and Columbus's son Fernando later declared that Columbus had corresponded with Toscanelli.

The increasingly well-read Columbus was also influenced by the Bible, which induced him to adopt his name, Christopher, which stood for "Christ Bearer," and led him to believe that he had a mission to conduct. Also helping to shape his world view were any number of works he turned to, including Pope Pius II's *Historia Rerum ubique Gestarum*, Cardinal Pierre d'Ailly's *Imago Mundi*, Pliny's *Natural History*, Plutarch's *Lives*, and *The Travels of Marco Polo*.

On August 2, 1492, Columbus's expedition set out with three wooden ships: the larger *Santa Maria* and two light, sailing boats, the *Pinta*, and the *Nina*. On board were 90 men, most Spaniards, many of them having been influenced to sail by a pair of friars. Columbus relied on compasses, astrolabes, hourglasses, maps, charts, and the North Star, to navigate the passage. By all accounts, he was expert at following natural indicators, including the behavior of birds, the quality of the air, the hue of the sky, the shape of the ocean, and the quirks of his own body. Within nine days, the Canary Islands were reached, where provisions were obtained and necessary repairs undertaken. The boats sailed again on September 6, riding the Canary Current, which sped them along. By mid-September, signs of life, including birds and seaweed, had been spotted. Early on the morning of October 12, a lookout cried out, "Tierra! Tierra!"

When Columbus and his crew landed in the Bahamas, believing they had reached the Far East, they encountered territory that Europeans did not know existed. Naming the island San Salvador, Columbus claimed it for the Spanish crown, although under medieval interpretations of natural law, only uninhabited terrain could be deemed the property of its discoverer. When Arawak Indians sporting gold ornaments were encountered, Columbus considered these generous people Indians. Within a few days, the fleet sailed away, reaching the Bay of Briay, off the Cuban coast, on October 28. Believing they had found China, Columbus nevertheless continued on to Hispaniola. Troubles developed with certain crewmembers becoming restive and the *Santa Maria* grounded in late December. Leaving behind about 40 men to search for gold on the reef near Hispaniola where the *Santa Maria* had been destroyed, Columbus sailed for home, taking with him several captured Indians.

That return voyage proved eventful, resulting in a separation of the remaining two ships and the arrest of Columbus's crew from the *Nina* on the Portuguese island of Santa Maria in the Azores. When Columbus threatened to wreak havoc, his men were released and they made it back to Lisbon, the same day the *Pinta* arrived. Received as a conquered hero, Columbus was rewarded with riches and named Admiral of the Ocean Sea and Viceroy of the Indies. Instructed to colonize Hispaniola, Christianize the Indians, establish a trading post, and continue his explorations, Columbus sailed again at the head of seventeen ships, sporting 1000 men, on September 25, 1493. On returning to Hispaniola, they discovered that the native peoples, who believed the Europeans mistreated them, had killed the men who had been left behind. Columbus founded a new colony, Isabela, located on Hispaniola's northern coast, where he left his brother Diego in charge. Increasingly, Columbus's attention was focused on subjugating the Indians, not exploring additional territory. Native peoples were enslaved and compelled to toil at the direction of the Spanish colony.

In 1496, Columbus finally sailed back to Spain, but his reception this time was somewhat cooler, as no gold had been found. Nevertheless, Ferdinand and Isabella sponsored a third expedition, which Columbus initiated on May 30, 1498, but his monopoly was rescinded. After reaching the Canaries, the boats diverged, with some heading for Hispaniola and others, following Columbus's lead, veering sharply southward. After encountering an island, which he named Trinidad, Columbus sailed through the Gulf of Paria to the coast of Venezuela and the continent he would call an "Other World." He later wrote in his journal, "I believe that this is a very great continent which until today has been unknown." Returning to Hispaniola yet again, Columbus found the colony to be troubled and rife with angry European inhabitants. Charges were leveled that insufficient gold and edible foodstuffs were available, and accusations delivered about Columbus's purported mishandling of colonial matters. In 1500, the Spanish crown sent Francisco de Bobadilla to bring order to the colony of Hispaniola. Columbus and his two brothers were enchained and sent to Spain to be tried, but were released by Ferdinand and Isabella.

To placate the increasingly hard-to-handle Columbus, the Spanish monarchs agreed to finance one final voyage. During that period, he was characterized as a "tall man and well built, ruddy, of a great creative talent, and with a long face." Blond-haired in his youth, Columbus sported white hair by the time he was 30. On May 9, 1502, Columbus led four caravels in an effort to find a passage to the Indian Ocean, supposedly locating Cuba and the "Other World" he had encountered. Departing the Canaries, the boats reached Martinique and then Santo Domingo, before skirting past Jamaica in the direction of southern Cuba. Then, they continued to the Bay Islands located off the Honduran coast. Later, Columbus went to the mouth of the present Panama Canal, unaware of the Pacific Ocean's proximity. A trading network was set up with the Indians in Costa Rica and Panama, who swapped a considerable amount of copper and gold objects. A less happy scenario unfolded when the local Guaymi Indians battled against the Spaniards, inflicting a considerable number of casualties. Columbus determined it was time to head for home, which he did on April 16, 1503. However, problems involving leaking boats forced him to remain in Jamaica for a year, but on June 29, 1504, the crew departed, reaching Sanlucar, Spain, on November 7, 1504.

Unfortunately for Columbus, shortly after he returned to Spain, his greatest patron, Queen Isabella died. The fifty-three year-old Columbus himself was in poor health, suffering from rheumatism, exposure to the elements, and poor dietary habits. After several months of recuperation, he sought in vain to have his titles restored. King Ferdinand did allow for arbitration to take place regarding Columbus's financial claims, which resulted in his receipt of approximately two percent of the wealth of the Indies. Beginning in late 1505, Columbus, due to illness and depression, was confined to the city of Valladolid. His sons, his brother Bartolomeo, and a good friend, Diego Mendez, were present when Columbus exclaimed, "Into thy hands, O Lord, I commit my spirit," and then died. He was buried in Valladolid, but his remains were soon transferred to a monastery in Seville.

Columbus's historical significance is virtually unprecedented. Thanks to his voyages and the Age of Exploration and Discovery he helped to spawn, the so-called Columbian Exchange unfolded, in which plants, animals, diseases, culture, and human beings were transported back-and-forth across the Atlantic. Columbus helped to usher in the modern era, while arguably setting the stage for the intellectual revolution regarding the earth's role and placement in the solar system that Nicholas Copernicus, Galileo Galilei, and Jonathan Kepler would bring about. On a less positive note, of course, the imperial developments that flourished from the late-fifteenth century onward resulted in wholesale assaults on indigenous civilizations and peoples and the fostering of ethnocentric and racist ideas that would be hard to dispel. The costs in human terms, just like the accomplishments that the Age of Exploration and Discovery brought about, would prove staggering.

Suggested Readings

Morison, Samuel Eliot. *Admiral of the Ocean Sea: A Life of Christopher Columbus* (1991).
Stannard, David E. *American Holocaust: The Conquest of the New World (1993).*

Johann Gutenberg

While he didn't invent printing or movable metal type, Johann Gutenberg created the type mold that enabled book reproductions to flourish in the West. Unaware of earlier Chinese and Korean innovations, Gutenberg devised a successful Western system of movable type that went unchallenged for centuries. His publication in 1455 of 200 beautifully constructed Bibles initiated a literary revolution that transformed Western civilization. His ingenuity made possible the spread of ideas associated with the Renaissance, and later the Reformation and the Enlightenment. How monumental was Gutenberg's achievement? How sweeping were the transformations that it helped to usher in?

* * *

Although biographical information about his early life remains sketchy, Johann Gutenberg was evidently born in the last decade of the fourteenth century in the German city of Mainz. His father, Friele (Friedrich) Gansfleisch, came from a noble family whose roots could be traced back to the thirteenth century. By the fourteen century, the family held an hereditary station known as *Hausgenossen*, holders of the household, as the keeper of the archiepiscopal mint, associated with church government. That favored position enabled family members to acquire certain skills pertaining to metal work. It was their responsibility to deliver the metal that would be coined at the mint, to produce different varieties of coin, and to hold a seat at the assizez or legal proceeding when cases involving forgery were presented. Mainz itself was a key center where many goldsmiths and jewelers could be found. In 1386, Friele married Else Wyrich, whose father ran a pottery shop, and the two had three children, including Johann, whose birth took place between 1394 and 1399, in the Hof zum Gutenberg. Friele Gansfleisch died in 1419, leaving behind his widow and their three children.

In Mainz, Gutenberg probably received instruction in metalwork from an uncle who served as master of the mint. Because he was a member of a patrician household, Gutenberg avoided any formal apprenticeship. However, economic or political reasons induced the family to leave Mainz in 1428, settling instead in Strasburg, where the family name was known. There, Gutenberg was received as a member of the patrician class, while also joining the goldsmiths' guild. Serving as a part-time teacher and operator of his own business enterprise, Gutenberg instructed his students and compatriots, drawing on various skills he had acquired, including gem polishing, the production of looking-glasses, and printing. Requiring investors, Gutenberg signed a contract in 1438 with Hans Riffe, Andreas Dritzehn, and Andreas Heilmann, calling for them to provide the necessary capital to fund a new enterprise he was engaged in. As indicated by a legal suit pertaining to his experiment in typography, Gutenberg was working on a "new art" that led him to present certain valuable "printing requisites." In 1437, Gutenberg also suffered a "breach of promise to marriage" suit initiated by Ennel zur eisernen Tur, a young aristocratic woman from Strasburg. Perhaps that action led to Gutenberg's departure from Strasburg in 1444.

In Strasburg, Gutenberg had been working on secret and costly experiments, undoubtedly involving typecasting and printing molds. The ink used in his endeavors was derived from materials early Flemish artists had employed. Most important, his techniques helped to quicken the pace of printing, hitherto a terribly taxing enterprise. Prior to Gutenberg's discoveries, each printed page demanded its own form, generally made of a wood block. Gutenberg reasoned that he could use and then reuse metal letters and letter molds. Movable type had been employed in Asia, but the vast number of ideograms precluded its general use. Lacking knowledge about earlier Chinese or Korean efforts, Gutenberg's ingenuity led him to invent the type mold that allowed for printing from movable metallic type.

Perhaps he was driven too by an awareness that a new middle class was emerging in parts of Europe, one that was more literate and desirous of acquiring the kind of knowledge that had previously been the monopoly of the nobility and the clergy. Undoubtedly, pressure had mounted on printers to produce larger numbers of books to satisfy that literary appetite.

By 1448, Gutenberg had moved back to Mainz and borrowed 150 gulden from a relative, Arnold Gelthuss. Among his early productions were the "Poem of the Last Judgment" and the "Calendar for 1448." Two years later he borrowed 800 gulden from Johann Fust, a banker from Mainz, to print a twin-columned, "42-line Bible;" Gutenberg put up his equipment as collateral. Gutenberg sought to mechanically reproduce characters employed in manuscripts. In addition to technical issues pertaining to type founding, he had to somehow replicate the exquisite calligraphy characteristic of books of his era. His earliest works suggest that Guttenberg managed to reproduce original script, and to artistically recast individual letters, while identically spacing columns of text. No other fifteenth century typographer could duplicate his precise lettering, making his volumes unique.

Working with a Parisian, Peter Schoeffer, Gutenberg struggled to design and cut type font that would suffice. As matters turned out, their font proved too large and thus prohibitively expensive because of the cost of paper and vellum (fine parchment). Forced to obtain a second loan from Fust, Gutenberg was compelled to take on Fust as his partner in the quest to produce the Bible. Employing B42 type—allowing for 42 lines a page—Gutenberg and Schoeffer completed the task in 1455, resulting in the Gutenberg or Mazarine Bible. This was both the first Bible and the initial book in Europe to be printed, a remarkable accomplishment.

However, at that point, Fust, displeased that Gutenberg had been printing other items as well, ended the partnership and brought suit to get back the 2000 gulden he had loaned, along with interest. The resolution saw Gutenberg relinquish the B42 type and some of his equipment, in addition to materials used for the production of the *Psalter*. Fust hired Schoeffer as his foreman and the young man later became his partner and son-in-law. Together, they established the leading publishing firm of Fust and Schoeffer. Meanwhile, Gutenbeg also soon lost his earliest font types to Albrecht Pfister in Bamberg. Turning to Conrad Humery, a wealthy and powerful political figure, Gutenberg was able to set up another printer's outfit. In 1458, after printing items like calendars, he put out the 36-line Bible. Relying on a new technique involving two-line slugs, through which he incorporated a pair of lines of text in a single metallic piece, Gutenberg sought to print the *Catholicon*, a popular encyclopedia, which was a voluminous work. Following Gutenberg's death, Dr. Humery reprinted the book, which probably sold quite well.

During the last period of Gutenberg's life, he could be found in the court of Archbishop Adolf of Nassau, having received a pension to provide him with adequate food and shelter and a tax exemption in early January 1465. This prevented him from deprivation in his final days, before he died either in late 1467 or at the beginning of the New Year.

Gutenberg's methods came to be employed by a growing number of printers throughout Germany, Italy, France, and Spain. It is estimated that some half million printed volumes, ranging from religious tracts to scientific treatises, could be found by 1500. In the process, ideas associated with the Renaissance spread, as would those identified with the soon-to-appear Reformation. The reproduction of classical works continued to fuel the fires of the Renaissance, while the publication of religious tracts carried word of the doctrinal clashes between Catholics and Protestants. Ultimately, Gutenberg's achievement not only furthered literacy and popularized modern science, philosophy, and political tenets, but served to provoke dissenting thought too.

Suggested Readings

Kapr, Albert. *Johann Gutenberg: The Man and His Invention* (1996).
Man, John. *Gutenberg: How One Man Remade the World with Words* (2002).

14

Chapter

The Reformation

Martin Luther

With his posting of "Ninety-Five Theses" on the door of the All Saints Church in Wittenberg, Germany, in late 1517, the theologian Martin Luther helped to trigger a religious explosion that transformed Christianity. Defiantly challenging papal supremacy regarding the affairs of state, Luther set in course the Protestant Reformation that also reshaped political developments. Hardly desirous of creating the schism that Catholicism endured, Luther soon found himself battling against those with still more radical Protestant ideas. Why did Luther usher in a revolution, rather than the reform of the Church that he sought? What was the lasting impact of the Protestant Reformation?

* * *

Martin Luther was born in Eisleben, Germany, on November 10, 1483, to Hans and Margaret Ziegler Luther. While Margaret was deemed modest and religious, Hans, a miner, was said to possess an explosive temper. Luther's childhood was marked by a lack of material comforts and constant beatings, delivered by both parents. Later, he declared that the "harshness of severity of the life I led with them ... forced me subsequently to run away to a monastery and become a monk." He attended a Latin school in Mansfield, where basic instruction in the Ten Commandments and Latin grammar was provided. At the age of fourteen, he enrolled in a school in Magdeburg, while the next year found him in Eisenach. As an eighteen-year-old, he entered the University of Erfurt, planning to study law. In 1502, he was awarded the degree of Bachelor of Philosophy and then took his master's degree. Among his professors were two of German's preeminent theologians: Jodocus

Trutvetter von Eisenach, the university rector, and Bartholomaus Arnoldi von Usingen, an Augustinian friar.

On July 17, 1505, the twenty-one year-old Luther entered the Augustinian monastery at Erfurt, and was ordained as a priest two years later. On learning that his son had gone to the monastery, Hans Luther purportedly exclaimed that a "satanic delusion had undertaken him." In late 1508, Luther entered the newly formed University of Wittenberg, where he studied for his doctorate and taught philosophy and dialectics. In 1510, he was recalled to Erufrt. That same year or the following one, he undertook a mission to Rome, which lasted five months, but the purpose of that endeavor has yet to be discovered. Back in Wittenberg in 1512, he was appointed as sub-prior, then named *licentiate*, and finally, dean of Carlstadt, after receiving his doctorate. In 1513, he was appointed lecturer of the Bible, while in 1515, he became district vicar, which put him in charge of Saxony and Thuringia.

Temperamental, neurotic, and brooding, Luther viewed himself as wicked and troubled. At the same time, he considered God to be angry and wrathful, but capable of being placated by "his own righteousness" and through the "efficacy of servile works." Enforced self-denial only seemed to exacerbate Luther's propensities to depression and a harshly critical reading of his fellow man. Original sin, he believed, ensured that man was depraved and lacking in free will. Only faith could save one's soul. Life, for Luther, was hardly about justice. Sin would necessarily be committed, and Christ was "the victor of sin, death and the world."

The issuance of the papal Bull of Indulgences in Germany proved cathartic for Luther. He evidently heard confessions of those who had either made payments to the Church, which would supposedly absolve them of the temporal punishment that sins demanded, or had listened to the Dominican monk John Tetzel preach about such developments. On October 31, 1517, Luther went to the door of the All Saints Church in Wittenberg and posted his "Ninety-Five Theses", a copy of which he also sent to the archbishop. Luther's manifesto was soon relayed to councillors in Aschaffenburg and faculty at the University of Mainz, who denounced it as heretical and demanded that action be taken against their author. This information, in turn, was sent on to the pope. As criticism mounted, Luther produced his "Sermon on Indulgences and Grace and Resolutions," which defended the "Ninety-Five Theses". Having been requested to do so, Johann Eck, a leading theologian, examined Luther's "Ninety-Five Theses" and indicated that 18 appeared heretical, were lacking in Christian charity, and bred sedition.

On August 7, Luther received a papal order instructing him to come to Rome within sixty days for a hearing. Luther staved off the mandate, on the grounds that he suffering from "infirm health." A meeting with papal legate Catejan, in Augsburg, on October 11, went badly but Luther subsequently agreed to display total submission to papal authority and to urge public loyalty to the Church. Soon, however, Luther reneged on his promises and his battle with religious authority intensified, as he acknowledged the worth of only two of the seven sacraments and insisted on the primacy of faith, not good works. He wrote "The Sermon on Good Works," contending that only faith could benefit the soul. Pope Leo, for his part, soon declared scores of Luther's writings to be heretical and his books were burned in Rome. Luther continued to escalate the sectarian battle, with his "Address to the Christian Nobility of Germany" urging the use of military force to compel the Church to examine grievances. "A Prelude concerning the Babylonish Captivity of the Church" called on clergy to revolt against Rome.

In 1521, Charles V, the Holy Roman Emperor, summoned Luther to appear before the Diet of Worms, which brought together princes, noblemen, and churchmen. After Luther conveyed his beliefs, Charles demanded that he recant. Luther refused to do so:

> Unless I am convinced by the testimony of the Scriptures or by clear reason (for I do not trust either in the pope or in councils alone, since it is well known that they have often erred and contradicted themselves), I am bound by the Scriptures I have quoted and my conscience is captive to the Word of God. I cannot and I will not retract anything, since it is neither safe nor right to go against conscience. I cannot do otherwise.

The Edict of Worms banned him. Managing to escape, Luther, now viewed as both a heretic and an outlaw, was spirited away by Frederick the Wise, Elector of Saxony. The prince sheltered Luther in a castle in Wartburg, where he continued his writing and produced a German translation of the New Testament, which helped to shape the modern German language. A letter to Pope Leo, "On the Freedom of the Christian," failed to placate the pontiff and Luther's excommunication soon followed.

The theological and doctrinal dispute that Luther helped to trigger resulted in schisms within the German Church. Similarly appalled by church corruption and other uninspiring practices—including those pertaining to actual services—large numbers of individuals began to break away from the Roman Catholic Church. Luther's gift was to be able to make his ideas accessible to lay people and clergymen alike, and he was fortunate too that the number of books in print in Germany leapfrogged during the very period that these religious controversies took place. Consequently, his writings were widely disseminated. Eventually, Luther's ideas were associated with a religious movement, Lutheranism, which many powerful advocates, including princes and free cities, came to champion.

Luther himself was hardly pleased with all the political and religious developments that began to unfold. In 1522 and 1523, the Knights' War saw members of the lower nobility—some, determined supporters of Luther—battle unsuccessfully against officialdom in southwestern Germany. The more serious Peasants' War of 1524–1525 may have involved up to 300,000 peasants in that same sector of Germany, as well as in central provinces. This uprising was also quelled, at considerable cost. The next decade saw the Anabaptists, a radical religious sect, grab control of several localities, in their bid to create a more humane society. Once again, this latest revolutionary upsurge was crushed. Luther tried to lend his weight to those who opposed such revolts. Indeed, he demanded that they be put down. Hardly a political radical, Luther called for worldly authorities to be adhered to, provided they afforded freedom of worship.

During the final two decades of his life, Luther continued to serve as the leading figure in the Protestant Reformation, to produce scholarly works, and to undergo personal transformation. In June 1525, he wed Katharina von Bora, a former nun. That same year, he published The *Bondage of Will*, which he considered his most important work. Criticizing Erasmus, *The Bondage of Will* declared that individuals could accomplish nothing that would lead to their salvation, which they could only acquire from God as a gift. Luther wrote *The Small Catechism of 1529*, which articulated Christian fundamentals. In 1534, Luther published his German translation of the entire Bible. His *Lectures on Galatians* (1535) brought together many of his most important tenets. On February 18, 1546, he died in Eisleben and was buried in the Castle Church in Wittenberg.

The religious movement Luther sparked helped to remake the continent of Europe. It resulted in the split involving Roman Catholics and Protestants and spurred nationalism. While associated with ideas culminating in demands for freedom of religion, Luther also offered commentary that could be drawn on by highly intolerant figures. After failing to win over Jews, he denounced them as innately evil, as "venomous beasts, vipers, disgusting scum ... devils incarnate ... Let the magistrates burn their synagogues ... Let them force to work, and if this avails nothing, we will be compelled to expel them like dogs ... not to expose ourselves to incurring divine wrath and eternal damnation from the Jews and their lies." Certain segments of the

Lutheran church later apologized for this anti-Semitism, while acknowledging it helped to make possible the Holocaust that began in Germany four centuries later.

Suggested Readings

Bainton, Roland Herbert. *Here I Stand: A Life of Martin Luther* (1995).
Oberman, Augustinus. *Luther: Man Between God and the Devil* (1992).

Ignatius Loyola

Founder of the Society of Jesus, Ignatius Loyola spurred the Catholic Church's self-renewal movement, the Counter-Reformation. Challenging the Protestant Reformation, Loyola's Jesuits coupled vows of poverty, chastity, and obedience to their parish, with complete fidelity to the papacy. Thanks to the Jesuits, the Protestant surge was somewhat held in check and occasionally pushed aside. The Jesuits particularly became noted as members of an outstanding teaching order. What drove Loyola to found the Society of Jesus? What led followers to identify with the Jesuits?

* * *

He was born Inigo de Loyola in 1491, the youngest of 13 children of an aristocratic Basque family, at the Loyola castle above Azpeitia in Guipuscoa, Spain. When he was sixteen years old, Loyola became a page for Juan Velazquez de Cuellar, who was Castile's treasurer. While residing with the Velazquez family, Loyola could often be found at court. Clearly concerned about his appearance, Loyola was fond of women, gambling, and swordplay. In 1517, following Velasquez's death, Loyola served as the Duke of Najera's courtier. At the age of thirty, Loyola found himself stationed as an officer protecting the fortress in Pamplona against a French onslaught. The Spanish commander considered surrendering his badly outnumbered forces, but Loyola convinced him to continue waging the battle. On May 21, 1521, he suffered severe injuries to his legs, caused by a cannon ball. The disheartened garrison allowed the French to take over the fort. Loyola, who had experienced a broken leg, was carried back to the castle of Loyola by French soldiers, who were impressed with his fortitude. His leg failed to heal and had to rebroken and reset, which took place without anesthesia. Although it was anticipated that he would not survive, the leg healed. Because of the way it had been set, however, it was shortened, leaving him with a limp.

While recuperating, Loyola asked to read chivalrous tales, which he enjoyed most of all. None were to be found, but books on the lives of Christ and the saints were brought to him. Deeply impressed, Loyola thought to himself, "Suppose I were to rival this saint in fasting, that one in endurance, that other in pilgrimages." At the same time, he continue to fantasize about martial exploits and winning the heart of one noble lady in particular. Eventually, he became aware that his dreams of chivalric conquests left him dissatisfied, but his thoughts about saintly figures afforded him inner peace. As he later acknowledged in his autobiography, one evening he found himself viewing "the image of Our Lady with the Holy Child Jesus," which made him recall his sins, particularly those involving the flesh, with disdain. Now, he focused on spiritual matters alone.

Departing from Loyola, he delivered a general confession at the Benedictine monastery in Montserrat, close to Barcelona. On leaving, he exchanged his rich apparel for a sack-cloth garment, sandals, and a staff. He also discarded his sword and dagger at Our Lady's altar. Throughout most of 1522 and 1523, when he wrote his first draft of *Spiritual Exercises,* pertaining to mediations about Christ and authentic Christian precepts, Loyola remained in a cave outside the town of Manresa. Mystical experiences there led him to believe that God could be discovered in all things. He eventually reached Barcelona, traveled by ship to Italy, and received permission from Pope Adrian VI to undertake a desired pilgrimage to Jerusalem. Although he sought to remain there, the Fransiscan superior instructed him to leave. Faced with the threat of excommunication, he finally agreed to do so.

Although now already thirty-three years old, Loyola determined to become educated so he could enter the priesthood to serve others. He was compelled to learn Latin grammar for two years alongside schoolboys in Barcelona, before he could study philosophy at the University of Alcala. His zealotry, which led him to teach others about the Gospels and prayer, resulted in his imprisonment for a period of 42 days. Under the Inquisition, unordained teachers were considered suspect. Loyola moved on to the University of Salamanca, but was tossed in jail after only two weeks there. This time, he was told to teach only simple matters to children. Departing once more, he went to Paris, where he studied Latin grammar, literature, philosophy, and theology. Conducting that which later would be known as the Spiritual Exercises of Loyola, he again instructed other students. In 1534, he obtained the *licentiate,* and the following year, his M.A. degree. In 1537, Loyola was ordained as a priest, but declined to say Mass for a full year, hoping to deliver his first Mass in the Holy Land.

Along with a group of fellow priests who had similarly taken vows of chastity, poverty, and obedience to the pope, Loyola traveled to Rome to seek papal support. Before arriving there, he experienced a vision in which God told Christ, "I desire you to take this man for your servant." On September 27, 1540, Pope Paul III sanctioned the Society of Jesus, with Loyola subsequently elected by the Jesuits as their initial superior general. The Church was sorely in need of champions to defend its ways against the criticisms that had unfolded since the Protestant Reformation had begun. In his *Rules for Thinking* with the Church (1541), Loyola instructed the Jesuits to "always ... be ready to obey with mind and heart, setting aside all judgment of one's own, the true spouse of Jesus Christ, our holy mother, our infallible and orthodox mistress, the Catholic Church."

From that point forth, Loyola remained in Rome, directing the operations of the Society of Jesus, whose constitution he devised. He drafted thousands of pieces of correspondence that were sent across the globe to Jesuits and lay individuals alike, as the number of member of the Society of Jesus mushroomed from less than two handfuls to a thousand. Jesuits established schools, universities, and houses across the European continent and in such far-flung places as Brazil, India, and Japan. In a letter to Holy Roman Emperor Charles V, Loyola indicated that education must be employed "against the widespread evil that flourishes in Germany. ... Universities ... by the example of their religious life and the integrity of their doctrine, attract outsiders to virtue."

Long troubled by stomach problems, Loyola experienced more of the same in Rome. He died on July 31, 1556, was beatified by Paul V on July 27, 1609, and was canonized by Pope Gregory XV on March 12, 1622. One of his closest compatriots, Luis Gonclaves de Camara, spoke of the man himself:

He was always rather inclined toward love; moreover, he seemed all love, and because of that he was universally loved by all. There was no one in the Society who did not have much great love for him and did not consider himself much loved by him.

The Catholic Church and the Jesuits both celebrate Loyola's feast day, July 31.

Suggested Readings

Caraman, Philip. *Ignatius Loyola: A Biography of the Founder of the Jesuits* (1990).
Idigoras, J. Ignacio Tellech. *Ignatius of Loyola: The Pilgrim Saint* (1994).
O'Malley, John W. *The First Jesuits* (1993).

15

Chapter

Rulers and Revolutionaries

Louis XIV

As ruler of France for 72 years, Louis XIV had a tremendous impact on his nation's domestic institutions. Remembered for his probably apocryphal assertion, "I am the state," Louis oversaw an absolutist regime that was the envy of monarchs across the continent, many of whom sought to emulate the French king. His ambitions also sparked an almost continual series of wars beginning in the 1660s and lasting almost to his death in 1715. What policies did Louis XIV implement in order to strengthen the absolutist state? What were his major foreign policy goals?

* * *

The child destined to raise French absolutism to its pinnacle was born in 1638 to parents who cared little for one another. Louis XIII and Anne of Austria had been wed largely out of diplomatic considerations and nurtured a mutual detestation for each other in the twenty-three years of marriage that preceded the birth of their son Louis. Since the mid-1620s, Louis XIII and his powerful chief minister Cardinal Richelieu had striven to lay the foundations for an absolutist Bourbon monarchy. The Cardinal's death in 1642 presaged the death of the king by only a year, and as Louis was only five years old, Anne ruled as regent with the assistance of yet another powerful cleric, Cardinal Mazarin. Though Mazarin assumed responsibility for the education of the future king, Louis was ill served by his tutors and matured with only a marginal familiarity with most subjects. Both contemporary and modern commentators have noted that the one area the otherwise lackadaisical Louis excelled in as a pupil was in his understanding of political power and how it was effectively exercised.

Louis' introduction to the trials of monarchy began in 1648 when the first of a series of aristocratic rebellions known as the *Fronde* broke out. The royal court's hurried efforts to escape from the forces mobilized by the resentful nobles who dominated the Paris *parlement* may have influenced the ten-year-old's later policies aimed at reducing the nobility to political impotence. Louis's opportunity to chart his own destiny came in 1661 with the death of Cardinal Mazarin. The young king informed his court that henceforth he would act as his own chief minister. For the rest of his lengthy reign, he steadfastly adhered to this approach, rarely entrusting any official with significant authority. He was equally his own man in his personal life. As had been the case with his own parents, Louis' marriage in 1660 to Maria Theresa of Spain was the product of dynastic considerations. Though Louis grudgingly accepted the marriage for state reasons, neither he nor his wife, who bore him only one surviving child, held any affection for each other; the long-suffering Maria Theresa once complained that throughout her married life, she enjoyed only twenty days of happiness and she failed to specify which they were. For his part, Louis sought the comfort of mistresses, sometimes maintaining more than one at a time and eventually marrying the marquise de Maintenon after his wife's death.

Affairs of state clearly had priority over affairs of the heart, however, and Louis busied himself formulating and implementing those policies that would ensure his absolute authority as monarch. Much of the work of administrative centralization and modernization had begun as early as the reign of Henry IV and had been augmented during Louis XIII's monarchy, so there was a solid foundation on which to build. No doubt mindful of the quarrelsome nobles of the *Fronde*, Louis continued his predecessor's policies of reducing the power of the French nobility. The Estates General, the national assembly last convened in 1614, was not called during his reign and provincial estates were scrutinized closely to ensure that they offered no challenges to the ongoing centralization of power. Louis also authorized special tribunals to hear allegations against overly ambitious nobles and several death sentences resulted from the trials of the mid-1660s. The status conferred by nobility was eroded by selling titles of nobility to wealthy commoners, imposing new taxes on the aristocracy, and by excluding nobles from important government offices. Perhaps most famously, Louis sought to subjugate his nobility by compelling their attendance at the new court at Versailles, where construction on new buildings began in 1668. The royal court moved from the Louvre in Paris, with its troublesome memories of the *Fronde*, to the new site at Versailles in 1682. Eventually, court life there was centered on highly formalized rituals and ceremonies calculated to emphasize the centrality and supremacy of the "Sun King," as Louis now styled himself. What little residual influence nobles might have came only from their proximity to their king. As one fawning courtier was said to have remarked to Louis, "Sire, away from Your Majesty one is not only miserable but ridiculous."

Any seventeenth-century monarch aspiring to absolute authority had also to be concerned about the challenges posed by religious authority and those who dissented from the state religion. Though a Catholic monarch, Louis was a staunch defender of Gallicanism, which held that the French monarch controlled the French church and in the 1680s, he saw to it that his bishops affirmed the French monarch's temporal authority in the face of papal challenges. Later wars against Protestant coalitions led Louis to seek a compromise with the Roman church over this contentious issue. Louis proved less willing to compromise over the issue of dissenting religious creeds, in part because absolute authority was more easily wielded in a nation in which there was religious uniformity. Accordingly, Louis felt compelled to move against the Jansenists, a Catholic movement that advocated a doctrine suspiciously similar to the Calvinist concept of predestination. Jansenism also preached an ascetic lifestyle, which the "Sun King" saw as an indirect rebuke of his personal behavior. Near the end of his reign, he succeeded in winning a papal bull against the increasingly influential creed. His greater effort, however, was directed against the French Protestants, or Huguenots. Though their religious and civil freedoms had been guaranteed by Henry IV's Edict of Nantes (1598), the Huguenots were a continual reminder to Louis that not all his subject shared his religion, a reality that he found increasingly unpalatable. As of the 1670s, Louis implemented policies calculated to make life in France intolerable for the Huguenots; in 1685, these persecutions culminated with the revocation of the Edict of Nantes. Several thousand Huguenots fled abroad, taking with them some of the nation's best entrepreneurial, professional and intellectual talent.

Beyond perfecting the absolutist state, Louis focused on strengthening the French nation. This was to be accomplished in part through the implementation of mercantilist policies aimed at building foreign trade, increasing exports and securing state revenues adequate to fund Louis's expansionist ambitions. Jean-Baptiste Colbert, whom Louis entrusted with greater autonomy than any other royal official, oversaw these economic initiatives. Colbert's efforts to organize and invigorate the French economy were ambitious, though they never produced the desired long-term results. Colbert's other major accomplishment was the organization of a modern French navy, part of a broader plan to transform France into the dominant continental power. To create this new military machine, Louis turned to Michel de Tellier, the Marquis de Louvois, who reorganized the French army along modern lines and increased its size tenfold within a decade. Marshal Vauban, a great military engineer, provided additional expertise, designing the fortifications that were so central to seventeenth century warfare. These individuals and others contributed to the creation of a French war machine that was crucial to Louis's territorial and dynastic ambitions.

Earlier in the seventeenth century, much of Europe had feared the emergence of a "universal monarchy," a dynasty dominating the continent through dynastic marriages, diplomacy and military strength, under the Austrian Habsburgs. While the outcome of the Thirty Years' War had ended that possibility, Louis XIV's France emerged to pose a similar threat toward the century's end. Indeed, Louis' ambitions lay behind the long series of conflicts that began in the mid-1660s and ended only in 1713.

Louis' initial objectives were the Spanish Netherlands and Franche-Comté, which claimed by right of the law of devolution. That entitled him, he claimed, as the husband of Maria Theresa, to these territories possessed by the recently deceased Philip IV of Spain. The tortured legality of the claim only highlighted Louis's baldly expansionist ambitions. Following a French invasion of the two Spanish territories in May 1667, the Dutch quickly ended their war with England and sought instead an alliance in view of probable future French aggression. Faced with opposition from the Netherlands, England and Sweden, Louis returned the Franche-Comté to Spain but retained some smaller Flemish lands. Angered by the diplomatic offensive organized by the Netherlands, Louis next planned a war against the Dutch, whom he derided as "a nation of fishwives and merchants." As preliminary to the Dutch War of 1672-79, Louis arranged for the nonintervention of nearby powers, buying off England's Charles II with subsidies and winning his ostensible military support. The success of French armies in their campaign in the United Provinces, however, awakened fears in the major powers about Louis's burgeoning ambitions. Fearing an anti-French coalition, Louis ended the war, giving up his Dutch conquests while gaining Franche-Comté.

Arguably at the height of his power in the 1680s, Louis cut an imposing figure among European monarchs. His contemporary Saint-Simon most effectively captured the essence of the man, replete as it was with inconsistencies. The Sun King was, according to the French writer, "the very figure of a hero, so impregnated with a natural but imposing majesty that it appeared even in his most insignificant gestures and movements." But unchallenged authority and the sycophancy of courtiers had also had an effect. "Louis XIV's vanity was without limit or restraint," Saint-Simon observed. This enormous royal vanity was fed by "the insipid and sickening compliments that were continually offered him in person and which he swallowed with unfailing relish." Such an ego was unlikely to be satisfied with limited conquests, and by the late 1680s Louis' obvious territorial ambitions had provoked the creation of the League of Augsburg, an anti-French alliance. The war of the same name broke out in 1688 and grew to international dimensions, pulling in England and taking conflict to distant continents. A general weariness brought peace in 1697, but all involved understood that it was more correctly only a temporary truce at best.

Indeed, Louis grandest ambition provoked an even greater conflict in 1701 when he sought to put forth his grandson Philip of Anjou as a candidate for the Spanish throne, soon to be vacated by the ailing Charles II. Fears of a Bourbon "universal monarchy" were revived and another anti-Bourbon coalition came together as the War of the Spanish Succession swept parts of Europe, the Americas and even Asia. Long years of warfare ultimately exhausted the combatants and the Treaty of Utrecht ended the last of Louis' wars of expansion. Though Philip was accepted as king of Spain, that throne was not to be merged with the Bourbon throne of France. Both France and Spain ceded numerous distant territories.

Louis XIV's legacy is mixed. France emerged from the War of the Spanish Succession with its extended frontiers largely intact and with its absolutist regime in place. Fifty years of intermittent warfare had brought domestic strains, however. War was a costly endeavor and Louis' subjects as well as his treasury were weakened by the decades of conflict. Louis' most fateful legacies to his five-year-old grandson, who succeeded him in 1715, were the economic and social costs of his conquests. Though Louis was said to have advised his heir to eschew grandiose palaces and war, the damage was done. As monarch, Louis XV was faced with massive financial problems and eroding absolutist structure, both of which laid the groundwork for the French Revolution of 1789.

Suggested Readings

Burke, Peter. *The Fabrication of Louis XIV* (1992).
Wolf, J.B. *Louis XIV* (1968).

Oliver Cromwell

An ardent Puritan, Oliver Cromwell was a member of England's Parliament who vociferously challenged the "Romish" practices of the Anglican Church and the policies of King Charles I. During the English Civil War, he was a notable leader of parliamentary forces and played a central role in the execution of the king. Later, Cromwell struggled to govern England first as leader of the Commonwealth and then of the Protectorate, a military dictatorship. What kind of government did Cromwell desire for England? How did he meet the challenges of leadership once he was head of government?

* * *

Oliver Cromwell was born in Huntingdon on April 25, 1599, the son of parents of modest means. Though Oliver was distantly related to Thomas Cromwell, a figure of considerable power in the court of Henry VIII, little of the great man's influence remained to benefit the family by the seventeenth century. As a young man, Oliver was influenced by his tutor Thomas Beard, who was a committed Puritan. Cromwell went to study at the predominantly Puritan Sidney Sussex College at Cambridge in 1614, moving to London later to study law. As of August 1620, Cromwell had married Elizabeth Bourchier and returned to Huntingdon to manage the small family estate following his father's death. As an educated gentry man, he typified a class that was attracted to Puritanism and politics, and in the late 1620s, he held a seat in the House of Commons, where he attacked the continued "Popish" practices of the Anglican Church. His primary attention, however, was devoted to farming and he moved to the cathedral town of Ely in 1636 to work some recently inherited lands. Prosperity eluded him, however, and as late as 1643, he sought unsuccessfully to immigrate to Connecticut, one of the Puritan New England colonies.

By the 1640s, however, Cromwell had undergone a religious experience, which drove him towards a more radical religious posture and frequent denunciations of the established church. Puritanism, which had been suppressed during the eleven years of the "Era of Personal Rule," when Charles I governed without parliament, gained renewed political force in 1640 when the beleaguered monarch recalled parliament to cope with the threat of a Scottish invasion of northern England. Cromwell now sat as the MP (member of parliament) for the university town of Cambridge, a hotbed of religious and political controversy. As a member of what came to be known as the Long Parliament, Cromwell stood with the Puritan radicals, demanding the "root and branch" reform of the Anglican Church and the abolition of the bishops, who were seen as an unbiblical remnant of the Roman Church.

He also sided with the political radicals, who challenged the "absolutism" of the Stuart monarchy and insisted on annual parliaments. In February 1642, when parliament proclaimed its authority over naval and military forces, Charles abandoned his capital for the north of England, and the English Civil War began to take shape.

By the summer of 1642, with England divided between supporters of the King's cause and that of parliament, Cromwell was assigned to raise troops in the Huntingdon and Ely areas and soon was commissioned as a captain in the parliamentary army. In an army short of experienced professional soldiers, Cromwell rose rapidly in the ranks, being promoted to a captain of cavalry in 1643. A lieutenant general by 1644, he led parliamentary forces to victory over a royalist army at the Battle of Marston Moor, where he won for his regiment the name "Ironsides." His most famous military role however, was as Lieutenant General of the New Model Army, where he served under Lord Thomas Fairfax. The New Model Army was an organization that reflected the revolutionary and egalitarian impulses unleashed by the civil war. Promotion came not from aristocratic heritage but from merit, and the troops were recruited as much for their ideological and religious fervor as for their military abilities. As Cromwell explained in a letter, "I had rather have a plain russet-coated captain that knows what he fights for, and loves what he knows, than that which you call a gentleman and is nothing else." The New Model Army also employed innovative tactics and strategies that were crucial to the defeat of the royal army at the Battle of Naseby in June 1645.

Military victory brought division among the parliamentarians, however, and the contentious debates led Cromwell to side with the army, which, unlike the Presbyterians, was supportive of religious toleration. At this juncture, Cromwell still favored a settlement with the king, as long as Charles would accept Cromwell's candidates as ministers and guarantee religious liberty for Protestants. Demonstrating a characteristic self-defeating duplicity that would later cost him his life, Charles chose this moment to flee to Scotland, where he gained a new alliance with his earlier antagonists. Consequently, Cromwell, the army and the vast majority of parliamentarians were convinced of the king's innate deceitfulness, and civil war was renewed in 1648. Cromwell further distinguished himself in this second phase of the war, suppressing a rebellion in South Wales, defeating the invading Scots at Preston and securing Yorkshire. 1649 brought new upheavals as parliament moved to realize the schemes of some of the more radical elements. In early January, the Commons, having already abolished the episcopacy, dissolved the House of Lords and the monarchy. Charles, having been returned to England by the Scots, was, at the insistence of Cromwell and the army, tried and executed for treason. The beheading of the king was, as Cromwell opined, "a cruel necessity." With England now a Commonwealth, Cromwell turned to the subjugation of Ireland and Scotland. Irish resistance was savagely crushed at the town of Drogheda, where Cromwell's forces massacred soldiers and civilians alike. The Puritan General, ever conscious of God's hand in temporal events, described the horrors at Drogheda as "a righteous judgment of God upon these." Scotland was subdued in similar fashion. He returned to London in 1651, where he turned his energies to finalizing the revolution.

The Rump Parliament, so-called because it had, over time, been periodically purged as it took on a more radical cast, now governed England. Support for this government steadily declined as its incompetence and apathy became evident. When the Rump introduced new measures to maintain the status quo by bringing in "persons of the same spirit and temper" to increase the number of MPs, Cromwell and the army acted. Believing all the new revolutionary liberties to be at stake, Cromwell moved to wrest authority from parliament. Confronting the stunned MPs in April 1653, Cromwell informed them that God "was done with them" and that there must be "other instruments for carrying out his work." In a final dramatic flourish, Cromwell dismissed the Rump: "You have been sat too long here for any good you have been doing. Depart, I say, and let us have done with you! In the name of God, go!" Soldiers cleared the House at sword point and the road to a Cromwellian dictatorship was opened.

Now relieved of the troublesome Rump Parliament, Cromwell set about laying the foundations for a truly godly government, one designed by the Puritan "saints" themselves to reflect a Biblical model of government. In July, a parliament of 144 Puritan divines, selected by the army and Puritan congregations, was called to bring into being Cromwell's pious vision. Remembered as the Barebones Parliament, after a member with the (surprisingly) not unusual Puritan name of Praise-God Barebones, the body failed to meet Cromwell's expectations. Like their more secular colleagues in the Rump, the members of the Barebones Parliament haggled over trivia and wasted precious time, leading to their dismissal in December. In the long course of the civil war and subsequent revolution, as the House of Lords and the monarchy were disestablished, the traditional constitutional structure of the English government was gradually rendered almost unrecognizable. There were now few alternatives left, and for Cromwell, the obvious expedient was military rule.

Compelled to establish a government with some arguably credible claim to legitimacy, army chiefs drew up the Instrument of Government, installing Cromwell as head of state with the title Lord Protector of the Commonwealth. Executive authority rested with a Council of State and legislative power in a single house comprised of "God-fearing men," meaning Puritans. This arrangement lasted less than two years, at which point Cromwell chose to rule on his own, essentially a military dictator backed by the power of the army. Through the 1650s, his new government drew little popular support, in part because the populace resented the activities of government agents who enforced Puritan law. Though Cromwell gave thought to having himself crowned as king, he abandoned the idea. The fundamental reality was that Cromwell, as chief of state, lacked the divine sanction of a monarch and any constitutional basis for his rule. While he promoted freedom of worship with only a few exceptions, and sincerely sought to create what he defined as a godly common-wealth, Cromwell proved willing to silence or suppress those who challenged his vision. The arbitrary nature of his rule may have been behind an effort in 1657 by some of his supporters to convince him to accept a crown. As monarch, Cromwell would be restrained by traditional rules and precedents. The Lord Protector refused this suggestion however and died with most of his powers unrestricted in September 1658.

Though Cromwell's son Richard sought to extend the life of the regime by succeeding his father, the army had little allegiance to him and the growing unworkability of the Protectorate compelled a change. In 1660, the Long Parliament was recalled to London to oversee the restoration of the Stuart monarchy. With Charles II on the throne, the rebels and revolutionaries of previous decades were discredited and, in some cases, marked men. Cromwell's body was disinterred and hanged, the treatment traditionally accorded traitors and rebels. For some years, his decomposing head was publicly displayed in London in a pole mounted above Westminster Hall, his body buried at the foot of a nearby gallows. The treatment accorded Cromwell's body prefigured the contentious debates that followed him into later centuries. The subject of considerable historical controversy even now, and especially in England, Cromwell is sometimes hailed as an advocate of religious liberty, but more often denounced as a religious fanatic who participated in the dismantling of England's constitutional structure, a development that led inexorably to dictatorship.

Suggested Readings

Frasier, Antonia. *Cromwell: Our Chief of Men* (1973).
Hill, Christopher. *God's Englishman* (1970).